MOVE IT!

STUDENTS' BOOK

SPLIT EDITION

3A

FIONA BEDDALL AND JAYNE WILDMAN

SERIES CONSULTANT: CARA NORRIS-RAMIREZ

Starter Unit

Grammar and Vocabulary • To be

1 Complete the sentences with the correct form of *to be*.

1 My brother *is* only ten, so he .... (not) at my school.
2 They .... (not) at home. Where .... (they)?
3 " .... (we) late for school?" "Yes, you .... ."
4 I .... (not) British. I .... American.
5 " .... there a mall in this town?" "Yes, there .... , but there .... (not) any good stores in it."

• Have

2 Choose the correct options.

1 I *have / has* a new pen.
2 *Does she have / She has* any brothers or sisters?
3 *He have / He has* some difficult homework tonight.
4 The movie doesn't *have / has* any good actors in it.
5 Do you *have / has* time for a coffee?
6 We *doesn't have / don't have* a dog.

• *Be* and *have*

3 Look at the picture and complete the sentences. Use the correct form of *be* or *have*, positive or negative.

1 He *doesn't have* blond hair.
2 She .... beautiful.
3 They .... curly hair.
4 He .... big.
5 He .... long hair.
6 She .... brown eyes.
7 He .... handsome.
8 She .... thin.

• Possessive *'s*

4 Complete the sentences with *'s* or *s'*.

1 She's *William's* (William) sister.
2 Those are my .... (friend) shoes.
3 The .... (dogs) legs are very short.
4 I can't see over the .... (people) heads.
5 The .... (man) hat is on the chair.
6 Look at those .... (girls) hairstyles!

• *Is* and possessive *'s*

5 Look at the *'s* in these sentences. Is it *is* or possessive?

1 The student's name is Hannah. *possessive*
2 He's in London.
3 Katie's good with computers.
4 The book's under the bed.
5 The book's pages are dirty.
6 Dan's mom has a new job.

• Subject and object pronouns

6 Choose the correct words.

1 She likes Matt, but *she / her* doesn't like James.
2 You can visit *they / them* tomorrow.
3 Please listen to *I / me*.
4 *He / Him* has a new car.
5 My grandparents don't live with *we / us*.
6 I want to help *she / her*.
7 Why do *they / them* like golf? It's boring!
8 When my brother plays football, we watch *he / him*.

• Possessive adjectives

7 Rewrite the sentences. Use possessive adjectives.

1 I have a very old computer.
   My computer is very old.
2 It has a small screen.
3 You have nice parents.
4 They have red hair.
5 He has a new T-shirt.
6 We have difficult homework.

● Common verbs

8 **Match the verbs (1–8) to the activities in the picture (a–h).**

1 fly *b*		5 sail	
2 eat		6 climb	
3 play		7 jump	
4 run		8 swim	

● Prepositions

9 **Look at the picture in Exercise 8. Complete the sentences with these words.**

around	behind	in front of	into	next to
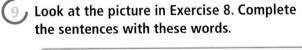 ~~on~~	over	under	up	

1 There's a tower *on* the island.
2 Someone is sailing .... the island.
3 A plane is flying .... the beach.
4 The sun is .... a cloud.
5 A girl is sitting .... the tent.
6 There's a CD player .... the girl.
7 A boy is climbing .... a tree.
8 His friend is jumping .... the ocean.
9 A ball is .... a chair.

● Indefinite pronouns

10 **Complete the conversation with these words.**

anything	~~everyone~~	everything
no one	someone	something

A Where is ¹ *everyone* today?
B They're all at the beach.
A Oh right! ² .... invited me, too. Who was it? Kate, I think.
B You're lucky. ³ .... invited me.
A Oh, I'm sorry.
B I don't mind. I don't like swimming, and I don't have ⁴ .... to wear at the beach.
A Come and buy ⁵ .... new at the store now! What about a new T-shirt?
B No. ⁶ .... in the store right now is expensive, and I don't have any money.

• Everyday objects

11 **Match the beginnings of the words to the endings. Then match the words to the pictures.**

1 maga	book
2 cam	et
3 lap	ter
4 wall	ns
5 note	zine *picture e*
6 pos	top
7 wa	era
8 swea	ter
9 jea	tch

• School subjects

12 **Complete the words (1–8). Then match them to the pictures (a–h).**

1 s c i e n c e   *picture c*
2 m a _ _
3 h _ _ _ _ r y
4 g e o g _ _ _ _ _
5 E _ _ l i _ _
6 m u s _ _
7 a _ _
8 l _ t _ _ _ t _ _ _

• Present simple: affirmative and negative

13 **Complete the sentences with the correct form of the verbs.**

1 She *doesn't live* (not live) here.
2 They .... (not eat) vegetables.
3 He .... (fly) to the Caribbean every summer.
4 She .... (watch) TV in the evening.
5 We .... (get up) at seven o'clock.
6 It .... (not work).
7 You .... (not know) Liam.
8 I .... (take) a shower every day.

Present simple: questions and short answers

14 Complete the questions and then answer them.

1 *Do you like* (you/like) science? ☑ *Yes, I do.*
2 .... (Jessica/learn) English? ☒
3 .... (we/do) PE on Tuesdays? ☒
4 .... (they/study) math on the weekend? ☑
5 .... (I/need) a new geography book? ☒
6 .... (he/teach) history? ☑

Adverbs of frequency

15 Write these words in the sequence.

| always | hardly ever | ~~never~~ |
| often | sometimes | usually |

0%
1 *never*
2 ....
3 ....
4 ....
5 ....
100%
6 ....

16 Make true sentences. Use adverbs of frequency.

1 I / late / for school
   I am sometimes late for school.
2 My class / listen / to the teacher
3 We / do / our homework
4 Our classes / interesting
5 I / take / the bus / to school
6 My friends / walk / home from school / with me

Numbers and dates

17 What are the missing numbers and words?

1 13 *thirteen*
2 ....   seven hundred and twenty-two
3 490   ....
4 ....   six thousand, one hundred and ten
5 3,412 ....
6 ....   eight million

18 How do we say these dates?

1 Jan 1 *January first*   5 Nov 8
2 Aug 3   6 Apr 25
3 Mar 14   7 Dec 23
4 Sept 2   8 Oct 31

Was/Were

19 Complete the conversation with the correct form of *was* or *were*.

A When were you born?
B I ¹ *was* born on July 2, 1997. But I ² .... (not) born in this country. My parents ³ .... in Kenya.
A Why ⁴ .... they there?
B My mom ⁵ .... a nurse there, and my dad ⁶ .... an engineer.
A ⁷ .... they happy in Kenya?
B Yes, they ⁸ .... , but there ⁹ .... (not) any good schools near our home in Kenya. That's why we live here now.

Opinion adjectives

20 Complete the adjectives in these sentences.

1 A lot of classical music is very r o m a n t i c.
2 Science fiction movies are very ex _ _ t _ _ g.
3 Mexican food is very t _ s _ y.
4 A lot of animations are very f _ _ n _ .
5 Rap music is t _ rr _ bl _.
6 This is an _ w _ s _ m _ football game!
7 Museums are b _ r _ _ g.
8 Skiing is e _ p _ _ s _ v _ .
9 Rock climbing is sc _ r _ .
10 A tarantula is a w _ _ rd pet!
11 A lot of children's TV shows are _ n _ oy _ _ g.

21 Give your opinion. Make six sentences, using adjectives from Exercise 20 and some of these words.

action movies	bowling	documentaries
fish	horror movies	jazz
judo	musicals	opera
pasta	rock music	skateboarding
surfing	vegetables	

Skateboarding is an exciting sport.

Speaking and Listening

 Read and listen to the conversation.
1.2 **Correct the answers.**

Ruby

1 Where are you from?
   I'm from ~~Miami~~. *Orlando*
2 Why do you live in Frederick now?
   Because my dad has a new job here.
3 When did you move to Frederick?
   Yesterday.
4 How old are you?
   I'm seventeen.

Tom

5 Who do you have in your family?
   My mom, my dad and my sister Ruby.
6 Which road does your family live on?
   Ash Road.
7 How do you go to school?
   I go by bike.
8 When do you leave in the morning?
   At eight o'clock.

 Act out the conversation in groups of four.

Ruby	Excuse me, where's room 27?
Ella	It's on the left here. We can show you.
Ruby	Thanks.
Ash	Are you new at this school?
Ruby	Yes. I only moved here last week.
Ash	Welcome to Frederick! Where are you from?
Ruby	Orlando, but my mom has a job here now.
Tom	Where do you live?
Ruby	On Talbot Road.
Ella	We live there, too—at number 72 Talbot Road. What about you?
Ruby	Our house is number 73!
Tom	Cool! We can see your house from our window. I'm Tom. This is my sister, Ella, and this is our friend, Ash. We're all fourteen.
Ruby	Me, too! Hi, guys. I'm Ruby.
Ella	Hey, do you want to walk to school with us tomorrow? We usually leave at eight fifteen.
Ruby	Sure! Thanks.

3 Complete the sentences from the conversation.

1 *Welcome* to Frederick!
2 What .... you?
3 I'm Tom. .... is my sister, Ella.
4 Hi, ... I'm Ruby.

Reading

4 Read the page from the school website.

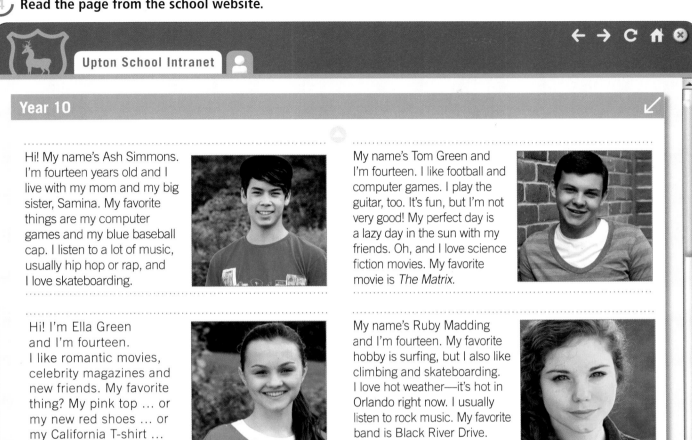

Upton School Intranet

Year 10

Hi! My name's Ash Simmons. I'm fourteen years old and I live with my mom and my big sister, Samina. My favorite things are my computer games and my blue baseball cap. I listen to a lot of music, usually hip hop or rap, and I love skateboarding.

My name's Tom Green and I'm fourteen. I like football and computer games. I play the guitar, too. It's fun, but I'm not very good! My perfect day is a lazy day in the sun with my friends. Oh, and I love science fiction movies. My favorite movie is *The Matrix*.

Hi! I'm Ella Green and I'm fourteen. I like romantic movies, celebrity magazines and new friends. My favorite thing? My pink top … or my new red shoes … or my California T-shirt … oh, I can't choose!

My name's Ruby Madding and I'm fourteen. My favorite hobby is surfing, but I also like climbing and skateboarding. I love hot weather—it's hot in Orlando right now. I usually listen to rock music. My favorite band is Black River Drive.

5 Read the website again. Copy and complete the table.

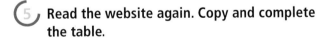

Name	Ash ….
Likes	computer games, …. , …. and rap music, ….
Name	…. Green
Likes	…. movies, …. magazines, new …. , clothes
Name	Tom ….
Likes	…. , computer games, the …. , …. movies
Name	Ruby Madding
Likes	…. , climbing, …. , …. weather, …. music

Writing

6 Make your profile for the school website.

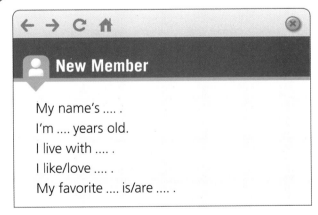

New Member

My name's …. .
I'm …. years old.
I live with …. .
I like/love …. .
My favorite …. is/are …. .

My assessment profile: page 127

Home Sweet Home

1

Vocabulary • Rooms and parts of the house

1 Match the pictures of the parts of the house (1–16) to these words.
1.3 Then listen, check and repeat.

Grammar
Present simple and continuous; Verb + -ing

Vocabulary
Rooms and parts of the house; Furniture and household objects

■ **Speaking**
Describing a place

Writing
A description of a room

Word list page 43
Workbook page 116

attic	balcony
basement	ceiling
driveway	fireplace
floor	garage
hallway	landing
office	patio 1
roof	stairs
wall	yard

2 Complete the sentences with the words in Exercise 1.

1 The *stairs* go up to the bedrooms at the top of a house.
2 You come into the house through the _ _ _ _ _ _ _ .
3 There's a bird on the _ _ _ _ .
4 The _ _ _ _ _ _ is next to the bathroom.
5 The red car is inside the _ _ _ _ _ _ .
6 There are boxes of old toys in the _ _ _ _ _ .
7 It's warm near the _ _ _ _ _ _ _ _ _ in the living room.
8 Someone is mowing the lawn in the _ _ _ _ .

3 Tell a partner about your home.

1 Do you live in a house or an apartment?
2 Describe the outside of your house or apartment.
   • Is it big or small?
   • What color are the walls and roof?
   • Is there a balcony, a yard, a garage, a driveway?
3 Describe the inside of your house or apartment.
   • Is there a hallway, an attic, a basement, an office?
   • What color are the walls, floor and ceiling in your bedroom and your living room?

> Our house is small. It has white walls and a red roof. There's a yard with a small patio. There's a driveway, but there isn't a garage.

Brain Trainer Unit 1
Activity 2
Go to page 58

Reading

1 Look at the photo. What do you think this building is for?

2 Read the text quickly. Choose the best answer.

1 Austin is a *teenager* / *adult*.
2 The building is *his bedroom* / *a complete house*.
3 He wants to *live in it* / *sell it*.

3 Read the text again. Answer the questions.

1.4

1 How are families in Europe and North America changing?
The size of an average family is getting smaller.
2 What are the disadvantages of big homes?
3 Where is Austin's bedroom?
4 What is 3.7 meters long?
5 What does Austin like about his house?
6 What happens when a building job is difficult for Austin?
7 Does Austin live in his house all the time? Why?/Why not?
8 Why is his house useful for the future?

4 In pairs, ask and answer.

1 Are many homes in your country bigger than they need to be?
2 Imagine your family in a house that is half the size of your home now. How is your life different? What is better? What is worse?
3 Would you like to live on your own in a house like Austin's? Why?/Why not?

Tumbleweed Tiny House company

Live Small

In Europe and North America, the size of an average family is getting smaller, but homes are not. In many countries they are getting bigger. Bigger homes are more expensive, and heating them in cold weather is worse for the environment. Many people believe it's time to think again about the size of our homes. Sixteen-year-old Austin Hay is building a home on his parents' driveway. It has everything important, including a bathroom, a kitchen and an attic bedroom with a low ceiling, but it's only 2.4 meters wide and 3.7 meters long.

"When I was a kid, I wanted to build a tree house," Austin explains. "But this house is on wheels, and that's a lot cooler."

Austin doesn't do any building during the week—he's busy with homework and playing baseball. But he usually works hard on his house on the weekend. "Right now I'm working on the doors. They're really easy, so my dad isn't helping me. He only helps with the difficult things." Austin is sleeping in his little house this summer. There isn't a fireplace yet, so in the winter he'll move back across the yard to his parents' house. And in the future? "College is very expensive in the US, but it'll be cheaper for me because I can take my little house with me. I can live in it anywhere."

Grammar • Present simple and continuous

Present simple	Present continuous
He always makes good food.	He is making dinner at the moment.
I live with my dad.	They're staying in a house without any adults.

Grammar reference page 108

1 Study the grammar table. Match the sentence beginnings (1–2) to the endings (a–d) to complete the rules.

1 We use the Present simple …
2 We use the Present continuous …
   a for routines and habits.
   b for actions in progress.
   c for temporary situations.
   d for permanent situations and general truths.

2 Choose the correct options.

1 Kat *doesn't talk / isn't talking* to me today.
2 I *always go / am always going* to bed at nine o'clock.
3 We *often go / are often going* to the movies on the weekend.
4 *I'm learning / I learn* about electricity in science this week.

3 Complete the phone conversation with the Present continuous form of the verbs.

A Hi, Ellie. How are you?
B Fine, thanks, Grandma.
A How ¹ *are you feeling* (you/feel) about your exams?
B Not too bad, thanks. I ² …. (study) on the balcony right now.
A ³ …. (the sun/shine) there?
B Yes, it ⁴ …. (shine). It's really nice out!
A You're lucky! Your grandpa and I ⁵ …. (wear) our coats in the house because it's so cold! What ⁶ …. (Callum and Leo/do)?
B They ⁷ …. (listen) to music in the basement. Do you want to talk to them?
A Actually, I want to talk to your dad.
B OK. He ⁸ …. (wash) the car in the driveway. Wait a minute …

4 Complete the text with the Present simple or Present continuous form of the verbs.

I usually ¹ *take* (take) a bath before bed, but tonight I ² …. (wait) on the landing. Why? Because my brothers Mick and Todd ³ …. (use) the bathroom for band practice. Most people ⁴ …. (not wear) their clothes in the bathtub, but Todd is different. At the moment he ⁵ …. (lie) in the bathtub with all his clothes on. Mick ⁶ …. (sit) on the side of the bathtub, and he ⁷ …. (play) something on the guitar. They usually ⁸ …. (practice) their band music in the garage, but my mom ⁹ …. (paint) flowers on her car in there tonight! I ¹⁰ …. (live) with the world's craziest family!

5 Make questions.

1 you / always / take / a shower or bath / before bed?
   Do you always take a shower or bath before bed?
2 what time / you / usually / go to bed?
3 you / often / get up / late / on the weekend?
4 you / listen / to music / right now?
5 where / you / usually / do / your homework?
6 you / work / hard / right now?

6 What about you? In pairs, ask and answer the questions in Exercise 5.

> Do you always take a shower or bath before bed?

> No. I usually take a shower in the morning.

Vocabulary • Furniture and household objects

1 Match the pictures (1–13) to these words.
1.5 Then listen, check and repeat.

alarm clock	armchair	blind	bookcase
closet *1*	comforter	curtains	cushions
dresser	mirror	pillow	rug
vase			

Word list page 43
Workbook page 116

2 Read the descriptions. Say the thing or things.

1 You put clothes in this. (two things)
a closet and a dresser
2 You can see your face in this.
3 You put flowers in this.
4 This wakes you up in the morning.
5 You put books in this.
6 This is on the floor. You can walk on it.
7 You sit in this.
8 This keeps you warm in bed.
9 You put your head on this in bed.
10 You put these on your bed or on a chair.

3 Which things from Exercise 1 are in your home? Make sentences.

There's a bookcase in the hallway, next to the living room door.

Pronunciation /v/, /w/ and /b/

4a Listen and repeat.
1.6

balcony	bookcase	driveway
vase	wall	window

b Listen and repeat. Then practice saying
1.7 the sentences.

1 My favorite vase in the living room is very heavy.
2 Why did you wash the windows and walls?
3 There are blue blinds in my bedroom.
4 I love black-and-white vases.
5 Do you want to have strawberry waffles for breakfast?

5 Say a sentence about the picture in Exercise 1. Your partner says *True* or *False.*

There's a blue rug on the floor.

False! There's a green rug on the floor.

Brain Trainer Unit 1
Activity 3
Go to page 58

Speaking and Listening

1 Look at the photo. Whose house do you think this is?

2 Listen and read the conversation.
1.8 Check your answer.

3 Listen and read again. Choose the correct options.
1.8
1 Ruby *wants / doesn't want* to move again soon.
2 Ash *likes / doesn't like* Ruby's new house.
3 Ruby's bedroom is *big / small*.
4 There's a computer in *Ruby's bedroom / the office*.
5 Ash *wants / doesn't want* to go into the living room.
6 Ella *likes / doesn't like* the town.

4 Act out the conversation in groups of four.

Ruby Thanks for carrying these boxes in from the driveway, guys.
Tom No problem! We don't mind helping.
Ruby I can't stand moving. I never want to see another cardboard box again!
Ash Your new house is really cool.
Ruby Thanks, Ash.
Ella What's your bedroom like?
Ruby It's a little small, but that's OK. There's space for a dresser and a little desk for my computer. Anyway, I prefer spending time in the yard.
Ella What's behind that door?
Ruby The living room. It has a big door out to the patio.
Ash Let's go out there now. It's a beautiful day.
Tom Hang on! Let's show Ruby the town first.
Ruby That would be great. What's the town like?
Ella It isn't very big, but it's pretty lively.
Ash Come on, then. Let's go!

Say it in your language ...
guys
No problem!
That would be great.
Come on, then.

5 Look back at the conversation. Find these expressions.

1 a question asking about Ruby's bedroom
What's your bedroom like? (Ella)
2 an expression describing Ruby's bedroom
3 a question asking about the town
4 two expressions describing the town

6 Read the phrases for describing a place.

Describing a place		
What's it like?		
It's	**a little** **pretty** **very** **really**	small.

7 Listen to the conversations. Act out
1.9 the conversations in pairs.

Ruby What's ¹ your bedroom like?
Ella It has ² pretty red walls and a white closet.
Ruby Is it ³ very big?
Ella Yes, it is.
Ruby What's ⁴ the swimming pool like?
Ash It's very nice. It's ⁵ pretty cold, but it has ⁶ a great café.

8 Work in pairs. Replace the words in purple in Exercise 7. Use these words and/or your own ideas. Act out the conversations.

What's your yard like?

It has grass and a lot of flowers.

1 your kitchen / your living room / your bathroom

2 green walls and a stove / white walls and a big sofa / pink walls and a large bathtub

3 a little small / very big / really small

4 the park / the library / the shopping mall

5 pretty small / very quiet / really busy

6 a lake / a lot of interesting books / some boring stores

Grammar • Verb + -*ing*

I prefer spending time in the yard.
Tom, Ash and Ella don't mind helping Ruby.
Ruby can't stand moving.
Do you like living here?

Grammar reference page 108

1 Study the grammar table. Complete the rule.

After the verbs *like, love, hate, enjoy, don't mind,* ....
and .... , we use verb + -*ing*.

2 Complete the sentences with the correct form of these verbs.

| do | get | ~~listen~~ | sleep | swim | wait |

1 I can't stand *listening* to rap music.
2 She hates beds. She prefers .... on the floor.
3 They love .... in the ocean.
4 We don't mind .... our homework.
5 Do you prefer .... up late in the morning?
6 I don't enjoy .... for buses in the rain.

3 Complete the second sentence so it has a similar meaning to the first one. Use the correct form of the word(s) in parentheses and one other word.

1 I think skateboarding is OK. (mind)
I *don't mind* skateboarding.
2 She never wants to have breakfast. (not like)
She .... having breakfast.
3 He's very happy when he rides his bike. (love)
He .... his bike.
4 It's better when we have band practice in the basement. (prefer)
We .... band practice in the basement.
5 They hate doing homework. (not stand)
They .... doing homework.

4 Make three questions with *Do you like + -ing.*
Then ask and answer in pairs.

Do you like going to the beach?

Yes, I love it. What about you?

I don't mind it, but I prefer going to a swimming pool.

Reading

1 **Read the magazine article quickly. Choose the best heading.**

1 Clean Up Your Room!
2 What Does Your Bedroom Say About You?
3 How to Have a Cool Bedroom

I **HATE** my room!

You can't always choose your room, but you can choose the things inside it. Because of that, your bedroom says a lot about your personality.

And we're not only talking about your favorite hobbies or your taste in music and books. Of course, a guitar behind the door or sci-fi stories in your bookcase give people information about you, but a careful look at your bedroom can teach them a lot more than that.

The colors in your room, for example, are very interesting. Does your room have bright colors on the walls, curtains, a rug or a comforter? Then you probably love trying new things. People with pale walls are often friendly and talkative, but people with dark walls don't like meeting new people. Black and white is a popular choice for people with strong opinions.

How big is your closet? A big closet often means that you are into fashion, but not always. It can also be a sign that you hate throwing old things away and prefer keeping everything behind your closet door. Someone with a neat room is usually cheerful, but someone with a messy room is moodier and often unhappy. The pictures on your walls say a lot, too. Generous people like decorating their rooms with photos of their friends and family, but if your own face is in every picture or you have more than one mirror, watch out! This shows that you are probably a little selfish.

So, before you invite your friends into your bedroom, think carefully. What message will your bedroom give them about you?

Key Words

| taste | careful | bright |
| pale | decorate | watch out |

2 **Read the article again. Answer the questions.**

1.10 1 What two things give information about your tastes and interests?
The colors in your room and the pictures on the walls.

2 What type of colors do shy people often have on their walls?

3 Why do people have big closets? Find two reasons in the article.

4 You are usually smiling. What does the article say about your room?

5 You like buying presents for people. What do you probably have on your walls?

6 What two things show that a person thinks only about himself/herself?

Listening

1 **Hannah is talking to a friend about her**
1.11 **bedroom and the article above. Listen and answer the questions.**

1 What does Hannah's bedroom say about her?
2 Why does she want to buy a lock for her door?

Listening Bank Unit 1 page 61

2 **In pairs, ask and answer. Is the article right about you?**

1 Do you have any bright colors in your bedroom?
2 Are there any pictures of your friends on the walls?
3 Are there any pictures of you?
4 How many mirrors are there?
5 Is your room neat?

Writing • A description of a room

1 **Read the Writing File.**

> **Writing File**   Linking words:
> addition and contrast
>
> **You can link similar ideas with *and*, *also* and *too*.**
>
> You're really talkative, and you like trying new things.
>
> The rug is green. The comforter is also green. The colors are interesting. The pictures are interesting, too.
>
> **You can link contrasting ideas with *but* and *however*.**
>
> I have some pictures of friends, but I don't have any pictures of myself.
>
> I love red. However, I don't like the bright red walls in my living room.

2 **Read about Matt's favorite room. Find the linking words.**

My Favorite Room
by Matt Davies

My favorite room is the office at home. It's a little small, but it's really light, and it's always very quiet. There's a big desk under the window. On the desk there's a computer and a lamp. There's a box of pens and pencils, too. In front of the desk there's a chair with green cushions. The walls are white, and there's a blue and green blind on the window. The carpet in the office is also blue and green.

I love sitting at the desk and watching all the people in the street. I usually do my homework in this room. However, when I don't have any homework, I like playing games on the computer.

3 **Complete the sentences with *and, also, too, but* and *however*.**

1 He has a big closet for his clothes *and* he has two big dressers.
2 My alarm clock wakes me up in the morning, and it can play the radio, ...
3 We watch TV in the kitchen, and we .... do our homework there.
4 I like playing tennis. .... , I don't play very often.
5 I have three pet lizards in my bedroom, and I .... have a pet snake.
6 There's a pillow on the bed, ... there isn't a comforter.

4 **Read Matt's description again. Answer the questions.**

1 What room is it? *The office*
2 What adjectives does he use to describe it?
3 What furniture is there in the room?
4 What color are the walls?
5 Are there other things in the room of a different color?
6 What does he like doing in the room?

5 **Think about your favorite room. Use the questions in Exercise 4 to help you. Take notes.**

6 **Write a description of your favorite room. Use "My favorite room" and your notes from Exercise 5.**

> **My favorite room**
>
> **Paragraph 1**
> Introduce the room and give a general description.
> *My favorite room is .... . There's a .... .*
>
> **Paragraph 2**
> Describe the furniture and walls.
> *The walls are .... and .... .*
>
> **Paragraph 3**
> Say what you like doing in the room.
> *I like .... .*

> **Remember!**
> • Use linking words *and, also, too, but, however.*
> • Use the vocabulary in this unit.
> • Check your grammar, spelling and punctuation.

Refresh Your Memory!

Grammar • Review

1 **Complete the conversation with the correct form of the verbs.**

A What [1] *are you reading* (you/read)?
B A postcard from my dad. He [2] .... (work) in Montreal at the moment, so we only [3] .... (see) him on weekends.
A [4] .... (he/like) Montreal?
B Yes, he loves it. He [5] .... (look) for a new home for us there, but my mom doesn't want to go. All our friends and family [6] .... (live) here in the US, and she [7] .... (not speak) any French.
A [8] .... (you/speak) French?
B Well, we [9] .... (have) French classes every day at school, but people in Quebec always [10] .... (talk) really fast. I [11] .... (not understand) very much!

2 **Complete the sentences with the correct form of these verbs.**

~~cook~~	eat	go	learn	live
not do	not listen	play	visit	watch

1 My dad usually *cooks* our dinner, but tonight we .... in a restaurant.
2 We .... about China in geography class right now. 1.3 billion people .... in China!
3 They .... to their new CD. They .... a movie.
4 She .... judo on Thursdays. She .... volleyball.
5 I .... to school in Connecticut, but today we .... a museum in New York.

3 **Make sentences and questions.**

1 he / love / play / basketball
   He loves playing basketball.
2 you / enjoy / run?
3 she / not mind / go / by bus
4 you / hate / lose
5 I / not like / learn / French
6 he / prefer / study / computer science?
7 they / can't stand / listen / to rap music

Vocabulary • Review

4 **Complete the sentences with the correct rooms and parts of the house.**

1 Come and have a drink on the *patio*. It's sunny today.
2 The light on the l _ _ _ _ _ _ outside my bedroom doesn't work.
3 The dog usually sleeps under the table in the h _ _ _ _ _ _ .
4 The c _ _ _ _ _ _ in the attic is very low. I can't stand up in there.
5 There's a big mirror above the f _ _ _ _ _ _ _ _ .
6 The grass in the y _ _ _ looks a little dry.

5 **Match the beginnings (1–5) to the endings (a–e) of the sentences.**

1 There are flowers in the *e*
2 On the floor there's a
3 He went to bed and put his head on the
4 She loves looking at herself in the
5 That window needs a

a pillow.
b mirror.
c blind.
d rug.
e vase.

Speaking • Review

6 **Put the conversation in the correct order (1–6). Then listen and check.**
1.12

a Do you spend any time there?
b It's a little small, and it isn't very sunny.
c It's very nice. It has really big windows and some very comfortable armchairs.
d What's your balcony like? *1*
e No, I don't. I prefer hanging out in the living room.
f What's that like?

Dictation

7 **Listen and write in your notebook.**
1.13

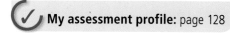
✓ **My assessment profile:** page 128

Geography File

Houses Around the World

1 Mongolia is near Russia and China in northeast Asia. The winters in Mongolia are very long and very cold. Many Mongolians keep horses. They move from place to place two or three times a year so their animals have enough food. When they move, their homes go with them. Their homes are called yurts, and they must be strong because there are often winds of 160 km an hour.

2 The city of Hong Kong, in the south of China, is located on a peninsula and two small islands. There are many mountains in Hong Kong, so there isn't a lot of space for houses. The buildings are very tall to save space. There are more tall buildings here than in any other city in the world. Forty percent of the people live higher than the fourteenth floor! Most people live in really small apartments, but they don't mind. They often eat in restaurants, and they don't spend a lot of time at home.

3 Belize is a small country in Central America. It is hot year round, with a wet and a dry season. A lot of people live in stilt houses near the ocean. This type of house stays cool because the wind blows through it. It is also protected from snakes and other animals because it is not on the ground. People often leave their car under the house, out of the hot sun. From June to November, there are sometimes terrible storms, but the ocean water doesn't come into the house.

Key Words

peninsula	space	stilt
blow	ground	

Reading

1 Read about these homes. Match the photos
1.14 (a–c) to the paragraphs (1–3).

2 Listen to a description of another home.
1.15 Choose the correct words to complete the fact file.

My Geography File

3 In groups, make a fact file about a home in another part of the world. Use the questions in Exercise 2 to help you.

4 Prepare a presentation for the class, including pictures or photos if possible. Then give your presentation.

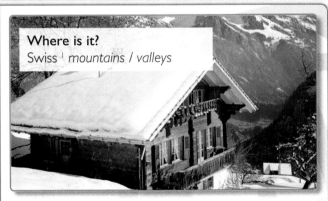

Where is it?
Swiss [1] *mountains* / *valleys*

What is the climate like?
[2] *warm* / *windy* in summer [3] *snowy* / *rainy* in winter

What is the home like? Why?
[4] *big* / *small* roof – protects the walls from bad weather
fireplace in the [5] *center* / *back* of the house – keeps people warm
[6] *patio* / *balcony* – people can enjoy the sun in summer

2 What's the Story?

Vocabulary • Adjectives to describe pictures

1 Match the photos (1–6) to the comments (a–f). Check the meaning of the words in bold in a dictionary. Then listen, check and repeat.
1.16

a It's an **interesting** photo of a famous place. It's very **dramatic**.
b It's a **boring**, **silly** photo. I don't like it.   *1*
c I love wildlife photos. This one is **dark**, but it's **beautiful**.
d It's a little **blurry**, but I like it. It's really **colorful**!
e It's obviously **fake**, and it looks really **horrible**!
f The clothes are **old-fashioned**, but the photo is **funny**.

2 Complete the sentences with the adjectives in Exercise 1.

1 My little brother is so *silly*. He's always telling jokes.
2 She often wears .... clothes. Red and green T-shirts are her favorite.
3 My cat moved when I took this photo, so it's .... .
4 It's very .... in here. Can you turn on the light?
5 Everyone said the famous photo was .... . Nobody thought it was real.
6 The storm last night was really .... . The sky was purple! But I hate storms—I think they're .... .

3 In pairs, ask and answer about the photos. Use the adjectives in Exercise 1.

> Do you like photo 1?

> Yes, I do. I think it's ....
> and ..... What do you think?

> I disagree. I think it's ..... .

**Brain Trainer Unit 2
Activity 2**
Go to page 59

Reading

1 Look at the title of the magazine article and the photos. What do you think you are going to read about?

2 Read the article quickly and check your ideas.

3 Match the photos (a–c) to the paragraphs (1–3).

4 Read the article again. Answer the questions.
1.17
1 What do the winners get?
The winners get a digital camera.
2 What is Lucas's photo of?
3 Where was Laine?
4 What is the weather like in Carrie's photo?
5 Does CLICK like Carrie's photo?
6 Does Jared like his photo?
7 Where were Jared and his family?

5 **What about you?** In pairs, ask and answer.
1 Do you take a lot of photos? What do you use—a camera or your cell phone?
2 Did you take any photos on your last vacation? What were they like?
3 Describe the best photo you took last year.

CLICK! Magazine — Young Photographer Contest

Every year at **CLICK!** Magazine, kids from all over the country send in photos for our fantastic contest. Here are this year's winners! The best photo in each category won a digital camera.

1 People
Photographer: Lucas
Subject: My sister

Lucas says: On August 5 we were driving to Canada for our summer vacation. I took this picture of my sister, Laine, in the back of our car. It was a long drive, and she wasn't enjoying it.
CLICK says: Lucas's photo is interesting and funny. You can see his sister's thoughts in her face. What was she thinking? How was she feeling? This photo really tells a story.

2 Places
Photographer: Carrie
Subject: A storm

Carrie says: Last month I was on vacation in Scotland with my family. There were a lot of storms, and this was a very windy day! The grass and the trees were moving. The picture is a little blurry, but I like it!
CLICK says: Carrie's picture is very dramatic. When you look at her picture, you can almost feel the wind!

3 Animals
Photographer: Jared
Subject: On safari

Jared says: Last year I went on vacation to the Serengeti National Park. I was really stupid—I didn't have my camera—but I took a lot of photos with my mom's phone. This one is my favorite. It was 3 o'clock in the afternoon, and it was raining. We weren't driving around—we were waiting for the rain to stop. That's when I saw the elephants.
CLICK says: This is a beautiful photo!

Grammar • Past simple

Last year I went on vacation to the Serengeti National Park.
I didn't have my camera.
I took this picture of my sister, Laine.

Grammar reference page 110

1 Study the grammar table. Choose the correct option to complete the rule.

The Past simple describes *a finished action / an action in progress* in the past.

We use the Past simple with past time adverbials, e.g., *yesterday, last week/year/Tuesday, two hours/days/weeks ago*

2 Complete the sentences with the Past simple form of these verbs.

> get   not go   not play   ~~see~~   take   watch

1 We *saw* the photo yesterday, and we all thought it was fake.
2 They .... on vacation last year. They stayed at home.
3 .... you .... my email?
4 I .... football last weekend. I couldn't because the weather was horrible!
5 She .... a photo and put it on her blog a few minutes ago.
6 ".... you .... the movie last night?"
   "Yes, we did. It was really boring!"

3 What about you? In pairs, ask and answer.

1 What did you watch on TV yesterday?
2 Did you do any homework?
3 What did you do last weekend?
4 Did you take any photos of your friends?
5 Where did you go on vacation last year?
6 Did you have a good time?

> What did you watch on TV yesterday?

> I watched the news.

• Past continuous

On August 5 we were driving to Canada.
We weren't driving around.
What was she thinking?

Grammar reference page 110

4 Study the grammar table. Choose the correct option to complete the rule.

The Past continuous describes *a finished action / an action in progress* in the past.

5 Complete the sentences with the Past continuous form of the verbs.

1 I *was waiting* outside the movie theater at 7 p.m. Luckily it .... . (wait/not rain)
2 At 9 o'clock last night they .... on the phone. They .... their homework. (talk/not do)
3 .... he .... football at 5 o'clock? No, he .... a game on TV. (play/watch)
4 At 8:30 a.m. she .... to school; she .... on a bus. (not bike/sit)
5 What .... you .... on January 1? .... you .... a party? (do/have)
6 At 1 o'clock I .... sandwiches; I .... pasta. (make/not cook)

6 Read about a day in the life of a wildlife photographer. What was happening at different times of the day?

1 9 o'clock / she / cook / breakfast
   At 9 o'clock she was cooking breakfast.
2 11 o'clock / they / look for / animals
3 1 o'clock / they / sit in the jeep
4 3 o'clock / she / take / photographs
5 5 o'clock / they / go back / home
6 7 o'clock / she / read / a book

Pronunciation Sentence stress

7a **Listen and repeat.**
1.18   At <u>7</u> o'<u>clock</u> she was <u>reading</u> a <u>book</u>.

b **Listen. Which words are stressed?**
1.19   1 What were you doing at 8 o'clock?
       2 Were you watching TV?
       3 He was doing his homework at 11 o'clock.
       4 They weren't playing football after school.

c **Listen and repeat.**
1.19

8 **In pairs, ask and answer about yesterday.**

What were you doing at 9 o'clock yesterday?

I was taking a shower.

Vocabulary • Adjective + preposition

1 **Look at these phrases. Check the meaning in**
1.20 **a dictionary. Listen and repeat.**

afraid of	angry with	bad at	bored with
excited about	good at	interested in	popular with
proud of	sorry for	tired of	

Word list page 43
Workbook page 117

2 **Match the beginnings (1–5) to the endings (a–e)**
of the sentences.

1 Karl is excited *e*
2 I'm afraid
3 He felt sorry
4 She was angry
5 Online videos are very popular

a with her brother because he told a lie.
b for Anna. She looked very sad.
c of snakes and spiders.
d with teenagers.
e about the game tomorrow. He loves basketball!

3 **Complete the text with the correct prepositions.**

Are you interested ¹ *in* music? Do you like videos?
Well, there are a lot of interesting video clips online.
Some are funny, and some are silly! People's home
videos, especially pets doing funny things, are
popular ² .... viewers, too. So if you're good ³ ....
making home videos, or you feel proud ⁴ .... a video
you made and want to share it, put it online. And
when you're bored ⁵ .... video clips and tired ⁶ ....
watching people doing silly things, just turn off
your computer and do something different!

4 **What about you?** **In pairs, ask and answer.**

1 Which school subjects are you interested in?
2 Which sports teams are popular with your friends?
3 What are you afraid of?
4 What achievement are you proud of?

Which school subjects
are you interested in?

I'm really interested
in history.

Brain Trainer Unit 2
Activity 3
Go to page 59

Speaking and Listening

1 **Look at the photo. Answer the questions.**

   1 Where are the teenagers?
   2 Who are Ruby and Ash looking at?
   3 What do you think the attendant is saying?

2 **Listen and read the conversation.**
1.21 **Check your answers.**

3 **Listen and read again. Answer the questions.**
1.21 1 What did Ruby forget?
     She forgot her camera.
   2 What does Ash want to do?
   3 What can't you do in the museum?
   4 What can the teenagers do instead?
   5 Why does the attendant stop Ash?
   6 Where does Ruby decide to go?

4 **Act out the conversation in groups of three.**

Ash	Is this your camera, Ruby? You left it on the information desk.
Ruby	Yes, it is. Thanks!
Ash	Do you mind if I use it? My camera is broken. I was taking it out of its case when I dropped it.
Ruby	Of course I don't mind. Go ahead … , but can we take photos in the museum?
Ash	Let's ask. Excuse me, is it OK if we take photos?
Attendant	No, I'm sorry, it isn't.
Ruby	That's too bad. I'm really interested in dinosaurs. But we can buy postcards. Look, there's a gift shop over there.
Ash	Great! I can buy some more chips. This bag is empty.
Attendant	Excuse me. You can't eat in the exhibition hall, but there is a café near the entrance.
Ruby	We can get something to drink there, too. Come on!

Say it in your language …
Go ahead.
That's too bad.

5 Look back at the conversation. How do Ash and Ruby ask for permission? How does the attendant refuse permission?

1 Do you .... if .... ? *Do you mind if I use it?*
2 .... OK if .... ?
3 No, I'm .... .

6 Read the phrases for asking for and giving or refusing permission.

Asking for permission	Giving or refusing permission
Can I/we .... ?	Yes, you can./ No, you can't.
Is it OK if I/we/ .... ?	Yes, of course./ No, I'm sorry, it isn't.
Do you mind if I/we … ?	No, I don't mind./ Of course I don't mind./ Yes, I do!

7 Listen to the conversations. Act out the conversations in pairs.

1.22

Ella	Can I ¹ stay up late tonight, Mom?
Mom	No, you can't. You have school tomorrow.
Tom	Is it OK if I use ² your cell phone? My phone isn't working.
Ash	Sure. Here you go.
Ruby	Do you mind if I ³ read your magazine?
Ella	No, I don't mind.
Tom	Do you mind if I ⁴ send a text message in class?
Teacher	Yes, I do!

8 Work in pairs. Replace the words in purple in Exercise 7. Use these words and/or your own ideas. Act out the conversations.

> Can I watch television, Mom?

> No, you can't. You have school tomorrow.

1 have a party / go out tonight / go to the movies
2 your camera / your laptop / your MP3 player
3 watch TV / play a computer game / play the guitar
4 get to class late / don't do my homework / forget my books

Grammar • Past simple vs Past continuous

(long action)	(short action)
I was taking my camera out of its case	when I dropped it.

(short action)	(long action)
I dropped my camera	while I was taking it out of its case.

Grammar reference page 110

1 Study the grammar table. Choose the correct options to complete the rules.

1 The Past continuous describes a *long / short* action in progress. The Past simple describes a *long / short* action. This can interrupt the long action.
2 We use *when / while* before a short action and *when / while* before a long action.

2 Complete the sentences. Use the Past simple or Past continuous form of the verbs.

1 We *were taking* (take) pictures when the museum attendant *stopped* (stop) us.
2 He .... (fall down) while he .... (skateboard).
3 She .... (do) her homework when her friend .... (arrive).
4 The doorbell .... (ring) while I .... (take) a bath.
5 We .... (eat) pizza when the movie .... (start).
6 It .... (begin) to rain while they .... (walk) to school.

3 Complete these sentences with your own ideas.

1 I was watching a horror movie when .... .
2 My friends were playing basketball when .... .
3 I was eating a burger when .... .
4 The lights went out while .... .
5 I heard a strange noise while .... .
6 We were sitting on the school bus when .... .

4 Work in pairs. Ask and answer about your sentences in Exercise 3.

> What happened while you were watching a horror movie?

> I saw a face at the window!

Reading

1. Look at the photos. Answer the questions.

1 What can you see in the photos?
2 Where are the people?
3 What are they doing?

Great Moments in History

This month *World Magazine* is looking at great moments in history. Do you remember these events? What about your parents or grandparents? What's the story behind the picture?

A V-J Day: August 15, 1945

Twenty-seven-year-old Edith Shain was working as a nurse in New York when she heard the news on the radio—the war* was over! All around the US, people were celebrating. Edith was celebrating in Times Square when a sailor kissed her. Edith didn't know the sailor, but she wasn't angry with him. A young photographer was in Times Square, too. He took this photo. A week later Edith saw the photo in *Life* magazine. She was surprised, but she was also proud of the photo!

2. Read the magazine article quickly and check your answers to Exercise 1.

3. Read the article again. Copy the table and complete the information.
1.23

	A	B	C
Event?	V-J Day	....	World Cup Final
When?	....	July 20, 1969	....
Where?	....	....	Mexico
Who?	Edith Shain	....	....

4. Read the article again. Answer the questions.
1.23

Paragraph A
1 Why did Edith go to Times Square?
2 How did she feel about the sailor?

Paragraph B
3 Why was the event on TV important?
4 What did Armstrong and Aldrin do on the moon?

Paragraph C
5 Why was the 1970 World Cup Final special for Pelé?
6 What was different about this sports event?

B Man on the Moon: July 20, 1969

Half a billion people were watching an important event on television. What were they watching? Astronauts Neil Armstrong and Buzz Aldrin. Armstrong was the first man to walk on the moon. "That's one small step for a man, one giant leap for mankind," he said. The two astronauts stayed on the moon for twenty-one hours and collected samples for scientists back on Earth. They left an American flag and some footprints. The flag and footprints are still there today!

C FIFA World Cup Final: June 21, 1970

More than 100,000 people were waiting in Mexico's Azteca soccer stadium. Italy was playing Brazil in the World Cup Final, and Pelé was on the Brazilian team. After the game, a photographer took this picture. It was Pelé's third World Cup win and the first major sports event to appear on TV in color. Millions of people were watching when Pelé lifted the trophy in his yellow soccer shirt!

* World War II (1939–45)

Key Words			
sailor	kissed	event	leap
mankind	stadium	trophy	

Listening

1. Look at the famous photo on page 61. Answer the questions.

1 What can you see in the photo?
2 When do you think the event happened? 1920s, 1930s, 1950s?

2. Listen to two people talking about the photo and check your answers to Exercise 1.
1.24

Listening Bank Unit 2 page 61

Writing • A description of a picture

1 Read the Writing File.

in the middle of the picture   in the background

the foreground   on the left   on the right   in the right-hand corner

2 Read the description. Find four phrases that say where things are.

My Favorite Photo by Jamie

I took this photo on my cell phone last month. It's of a family vacation in Europe with my parents, my sisters, Tara and Marie and my cousin, Joe. We took our dog, Spot, with us, and Joe brought his dog, Rex. The house in the background is Blenheim Palace. It's a little blurry, but it looks dramatic!

Joe and Rex are on the right of the picture. Rex was excited about some birds in a tree. He was barking and Joe was telling him to be quiet. Marie and Tara were laughing because Rex wasn't listening. That's Spot in the foreground of the picture, and Mom and Dad are in the background. Dad was taking a video with his new video camera.

I like this photo because it's funny, and everyone looks happy!

3 Look at Jamie's photo. Are the statements true (T) or false (F)?

1 There's a dog in the left-hand corner. *F*
2 There are two people in the center of the picture.
3 There's a palace in the background.
4 There's a man with a video camera on the right.
5 There's a small dog in the foreground.
6 There's a girl on the left.

4 Read the description again. Answer the questions.

1 Where were Jamie and his family?
  They were at Blenheim Palace.
2 When did they go there?
3 Why was Rex barking?
4 What was Jamie's dad doing?
5 Why does Jamie like the photo?

5 Choose an interesting photo of your family or friends. Ask yourself these questions. Take notes.

1 Where is it and why were you there?
2 Who/What is in the photo?
3 Where are the different people in the photo?
4 What were they doing?
5 Why do you like the photo?

6 Write a description of your favorite picture or photo. Use "My favorite photo" and your notes from Exercise 5.

My favorite photo

1 Introduction: when, where and who
  I took this photo .... (when?). I was .... (where?) .... (who with?) .... .
2 Description
  • what you can see in the photo
  .... is on the right of the picture and .... . In the background, there is/are .... .
  • what the people were doing
  My parents/brother/cousin was/were .... .
3 Conclusion: Why you like the photo

Remember!
- Say where things and people are in your photo.
- Say what people were doing.
- Use the vocabulary in this unit.
- Check your grammar, spelling and punctuation.

Refresh Your Memory!

Grammar • Review

1 Complete the sentences with the Past simple form of these verbs.

> go ~~have~~ make not do not write see send

1 *Did* they *have* English class this morning?
2 I .... you a text message five minutes ago.
3 We .... to the movies last weekend.
4 I .... my homework last night. I was very tired.
5 .... you .... some sandwiches for lunch?
6 She .... her blog last weekend. She didn't have time.
7 He .... a dramatic photo in the newspaper yesterday.

2 Complete the story with the Past continuous form of the verbs.

It was 4:30 p.m. and I ¹ *was sitting* (sit) on the school bus with my friend Emma. We ² .... (not talk) because Emma ³ .... (read) a magazine. I ⁴ .... (look) out the window. It ⁵ .... (rain), and people ⁶ .... (walk) down the street. A girl and a boy ⁷ .... (stand) near the bus stop, and they ⁸ .... (laugh). The boy ⁹ .... (not carry) an umbrella, and his hair was wet. He ¹⁰ .... (hold) the girl's hand. I recognized the boy—it was Emma's boyfriend! Then I looked at Emma. She ¹¹ .... (not read) her magazine; she ¹² .... (look) out the window, and she ¹³ .... (not smile).

3 Choose the correct options.

Ben I ¹ *called / was calling* you last night. Where were you?
Nina I was at home all evening. What time ² *did you call / were you calling*?
Ben At 8 o'clock. The phone ³ *rang / was ringing* for a long time!
Nina That's funny. I ⁴ *didn't hear / wasn't hearing* it.
Ben ⁵ *Did you sleep / Were you sleeping*?
Nina No, I wasn't. I wasn't tired!
Ben Then what ⁶ *did you do / were you doing*?
Nina Ah, I remember. I ⁷ *listened / was listening* to some music on my MP3 player.

Vocabulary • Review

4 Correct the sentences. Use these words.

> dark   ~~fake~~   horrible
> interesting old-fashioned silly

1 That's a cheap diamond ring. It's probably **real.** *fake*
2 I love wildlife photos. They're often really **boring.**
3 Matt was **nice** to Sue. He really upset her.
4 It's six o'clock in the evening. It's already **light** outside.
5 It's **sensible** to ride a bike without a helmet.
6 My grandmother's apartment is very **modern.**

5 Complete the sentences with these adjectives.

> afraid   angry   bad   bored
> ~~excited~~ interested popular tired

1 Paolo is very *excited* about his vacation.
2 They were .... with the TV show. It wasn't interesting at all.
3 I'm .... at math. I never get good grades on my homework.
4 Magazines are always .... with girls.
5 Guess what?! Joel is .... of mice!
6 Are you .... in baseball?
7 I'm .... of homework. There's too much to do.
8 I was .... with my brother because he ate my pizza.

Speaking • Review

6 Put the conversation in the correct order (1–6).
1.25 Then listen and check.

a Can I have a party on my birthday? *1*
b Yes, I do! It's very expensive!
c Do you mind if I take the whole class?
d No, it isn't. You can go to a pizza place.
e Great! Is it OK if I have the party at home, with my friends?
f Hmm … OK. Yes, you can.

Dictation

7 Listen and write in your notebook.
1.26

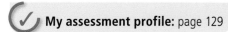

✓ **My assessment profile:** page 129

Kieron Williamson's Profile

👤 **Age**
12 years old

Home country
United Kingdom

My favorite things …
painting, soccer, watching TV, computer games

Young Artist

Kieron's Paintings

He's a famous English artist. He is in the newspapers and on TV, and all the tickets for his last exhibition sold out in fourteen minutes! He's called the new "Picasso" or the "mini-Matisse," and he's only twelve years old. Meet Kieron Williamson.

Kieron was born in 2002 in a town in southeastern England. He lives with his mom, dad and little sister, Billie-Jo. Kieron is a typical boy. He's good at computer games, and he watches TV; he's interested in soccer, and he likes riding his bike. He's also a brilliant artist.

It all started on a family vacation when he was five years old. He was playing on the beach when he saw some boats. He asked his parents for a drawing pad, and the next day he began to draw pictures of the boats. At first his drawings weren't great, but then he started to add background scenery, hills and houses. His pictures got better and better, and he began to ask his parents for advice. Kieron's mom and dad are not artists, so they asked a local artist for help. She gave Kieron lessons, and in August 2009, he had his first exhibition.

Kieron works hard at his art. He gets up at 6 o'clock every morning and paints. His pictures are of the countryside around his town. They're dramatic and colorful, and he paints four or five every week.

People all over the world love Kieron's paintings—and a lot of people are collecting them, so now they cost more than $1,700 each.

Key Words

exhibition	sold out	drawing pad
scenery	countryside	

Reading 🔊

1 **Read Kieron's profile. Complete the sentences.**

1 Kieron comes from …. .
2 He's …. old.
3 He likes playing …. and …. .

2 **Read the article. Answer the questions.**

1.27 1 Which artists is Kieron sometimes compared to?
He's compared to Picasso and Matisse.
2 Who does he live with?
3 How old was he when he started painting?
4 What was his first painting of?
5 How did his paintings change?
6 Who helped him develop his hobby?
7 What are his paintings like?
8 How much do Kieron's pictures cost?

Class discussion

1 Do you know any famous artists from your country?
2 How old were they when they started painting?
3 Do you know any paintings by Picasso or Matisse? What are they like?

3 It's a Bargain!

Grammar
Comparatives and superlatives; *too* and *enough*; *much, many, a lot of*

Vocabulary
Shopping nouns;
Money verbs

Speaking
Asking for help

Writing
A customer review

Word list page 43
Workbook page 118

Vocabulary • Shopping nouns

1 Match the pictures (1–15) to these words. Then listen, check and repeat.

1.28

ATM
bargain
bill
change
coin
customer
line
mall
market stand
price *1*
products
sale
salesperson
shopping basket
vendor

2 Complete the conversation with the words in Exercise 1.

Dean This is my favorite store in the ¹ *mall*.
Louis I love this coat, but how much is it?
Dean Ask the ² .... . She'll know.
Louis Oh! It's $17. It's on ³ .... for half price.
Dean It's a ⁴ .... ! Are you going to buy it?
Louis Yes, but I need to go to the ⁵ .... first. I only have a ⁶ .... or two, and I can't buy a coat with that!
Dean But there's always a long ⁷ .... at the ATM. Here's a twenty-dollar ⁸ .... . You can get some money later.

3 Complete the sentences with the words in Exercise 1.

1 The *price* of gas is very high.
2 This grocery store sells really good ....—they often buy from the local farmers.
3 Salespeople should always make sure they give the .... the correct .... when they buy something.

4 In pairs, ask and answer about your local area.

1 Where or when are there good bargains?
2 Which stores have friendly salespeople?
3 Where or when are there often lines?

Brain Trainer Unit 3
Activity 2
Go to page 59

Reading

1 Look at the photos. Do you think these statements are true (T) or false (F)?

1 The market is very old. *T*
2 Now it's only popular with older people.
3 It sells fresh food.
4 The prices are high.

2 Read the magazine article and check your answers to Exercise 1.

1.29

3 Read the article again. Match the headings (A–D) to the paragraphs (1–4).

A The market has a long history.
B Today that is difficult to believe.
C Shopping is often more interesting at the market, too.
D Haymarket vendors have plenty of loyal customers. *1*

4 Answer the questions.

1 What are Haymarket vendors happy about?
   Their market is becoming more popular.
2 What do locals like about Haymarket?
3 Why did people think the market might disappear?
4 What does Nick like about the products at the market?
5 What advice does Stacy give about the food from the market?

5 What about you? Answer the questions.

1 What are the markets like in your area?
2 How often do you go to a market?
3 What do you buy there?
4 What do you like/dislike about markets?

News   Boston

Boston Market Wins More Customers

Haymarket vendors have a reason to celebrate. Their market is becoming more popular than ever.

1 .... "This is the busiest market in Boston!" says Vicky Green at her fruit stand. "All the locals come here because it's very close to downtown. It also has convenient hours and the best prices in Boston!"

2 .... For hundreds of years, Haymarket has been the best place to buy fruits and vegetables in Boston. Vendors started gathering in this area of Boston's North End in the mid-1700s. The market grew larger in the nineteenth and twentieth centuries, but almost disappeared when highway construction disrupted the street in the 1990s.

3 .... The street is now filled with produce stands selling fruits and vegetables from all over the world. And customers love it. "Prices here are often cheaper

than in the grocery store, so you can find some great bargains," explains Nick Baines, 16. This is because vendors sell the produce that nearby

wholesalers weren't able to sell to grocery stores. "Just remember that the fruits and vegetables are usually very ripe," says Stacy Mills, 30, "so you need to eat them soon. But you can get a lot of produce for a great price. And the vendors are much friendlier than salespeople in a supermarket."

4 .... "In every grocery store you always find the same products," says Eileen Fisher, 21. "I prefer Haymarket because I can get some really exotic food here, for example, from Asia or North Africa. And there are many market stands to choose from."

The future has never looked better for Haymarket. It has truly become a Boston tradition!

Grammar • Comparatives and superlatives

Adjective	Comparative	Superlative
cheap	cheaper	cheapest
nice	nicer	nicest
big	bigger	biggest
friendly	friendlier	friendliest
interesting	more interesting	most interesting
good	better	best
bad	worse	worst
far	farther	farthest

Market vendors are friendlier than salespeople.
Haymarket is the busiest market in Boston!

Grammar reference page 112

1 Study the grammar table and the examples. Complete the rules with *comparative* or *superlative*.

1 We compare two people or things with the .... .
2 We compare one person or thing to the rest of its group with the .... .
3 We use *the* before the .... .
4 We use *than* after the .... .

2 Complete the sentences with the correct form of the adjectives.

1 We're *hungrier* (hungry) than you.
2 August is the .... (hot) month of the year.
3 It is the .... (large) market in Boston.
4 The T-shirt is .... (clean) than the jacket.
5 My sister's .... (selfish) than my brother.
6 This is the .... (bad) day of my life!

3 Complete the text with the correct form of the adjectives.

The [1] *most popular* (popular) markets in Thailand are on water, and the stands are boats. Taling Chan is the [2] .... (good) market near the city of Bangkok, but the [3] .... (big) and [4] .... (busy) market in Thailand is at Ratchaburi. It is [5] .... (far) from Bangkok than Taling Chan, and prices there are [6] .... (expensive) than prices in other places. Why? Because this market is one of the [7] .... (famous) and [8] .... (exciting) markets in the world!

• *Too* and *enough*

The jeans are too expensive.
The jeans aren't cheap enough.
I don't have enough money for the jeans.

Grammar reference page 112

4 Study the grammar table. Complete the rules with *too* or *enough*.

1 We use .... + adjective.
2 We use (*not*) adjective + ...
3 We use .... + noun.

5 Make sentences and questions.

1 aren't / people / There / enough
   There aren't enough people.
2 you / too / tired / Are / ?
3 fast / enough / It / isn't
4 She / too / works / always / hard

6 Complete the second sentence so it means the same as the first. Use the word in parentheses.

1 That color is too bright. (dark)
   That color *isn't dark enough*.
2 The shopping basket is too heavy. (light)
   The shopping basket .... .
3 The movie wasn't exciting enough for me. (boring)
   The movie .... for me.
4 Our baseball team is too small. (players)
   We don't have .... on our baseball team.
5 The library is never quiet enough. (noisy)
   The library is always .... .

7 What about you? Make sentences about different stores, shopping areas or markets where you live. Use comparatives, superlatives, *too* and *enough*. Use some of these adjectives.

big	busy	cheap	cool
expensive	good	interesting	noisy
old	quiet	small	

The mall is busiest on Saturdays.

There aren't enough clothing stores downtown.

Vocabulary • Money verbs

1 Match the pictures (1–12) to these verb pairs.
1.30 **Then listen, check and repeat.**

buy/sell *1–2*	cost/afford
lend/borrow	pay in cash/pay by credit card
save/spend	win/earn

Word list page 43
Workbook page 118

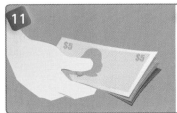

2 Complete the sentences with the correct verbs.

borrow/lend	~~cost/afford~~	in cash/by credit card
saved/spent	sells/buys	won/earns

1 The DVDs *cost* $20. I can't *afford* one. I don't have enough money.
2 The vendor .... fruit and vegetables. The customer .... her fruit from him.
3 Sam took out a bill from his wallet and paid for the sandwiches .... . Ellie didn't have any cash, so she paid for her lunch .... .
4 They sometimes .... their dad's laptop. But he doesn't always .... it to them.
5 Tara .... her money in the bank, so she has $500 now. Todd .... all his money on computer games, so he doesn't have any money now.
6 Daniel .... $100 in a contest last week. Olivia only .... $100 a week.

Pronunciation /ɔ/ and /oʊ/

3a Listen and repeat.
1.31

/ɔ/	/oʊ/
cost	go
long	home
on	show

b Listen and repeat. Then practice saying
1.32 **the sentences.**

1 Go home on the boat.
2 Can I borrow your orange coat?
3 The vendor sold me some old posters.

4 Match the beginnings (1–5) to the endings (a–e) of the sentences.

1 My favorite store sells
2 I usually spend my money
3 I sometimes borrow money
4 I usually pay for new clothes
5 If I can't afford something nice, I

a save for it.
b by credit card.
c pet snakes.
d from my dad.
e on DVDs.

5 Look at the sentence beginnings (1–5) in Exercise 4. Complete the sentences so they are true for you.

Brain Trainer Unit 3
Activity 3
Go to page 59

Speaking and Listening

1 Look at the photo. What does Ella want to buy?

2 Listen and read the conversation.
1.33 Check your answer.

3 Listen and read again. Answer the questions.
1.33
1 What help does Tom give Ella?
   He helps her with her bags.
2 Why does Ella want the T-shirt?
3 When does Ella want to buy the T-shirt?
4 Can the salesperson save the T-shirt for Ella?
5 Why does Ella ask Tom about his money?
6 Does Tom think the T-shirt is a bargain?

4 Act out the conversation in groups of three.

Ella	Hey, Tom. Can you give me a hand with these bags?
Tom	Sure.
Ella	Thanks. I want to look at these T-shirts.
Tom	But you have a lot of T-shirts, Ella. You don't need a new one.
Ella	I don't have many nice T-shirts. These are nicer than all my clothes at home. Oh look, there's the salesperson … Excuse me, would you mind saving this for me until next week?
Salesperson	Sorry, I can't. It's against the rules.
Ella	That's too bad. Er, Tom … how much money do you have?
Tom	Why?
Ella	Well, I can't afford any new clothes right now. Could you lend me some money?
Tom	No problem. How much?
Ella	$30.
Tom	$30 is too much money for one T-shirt!
Ella	But for $30 I can buy five T-shirts.
Tom	Oh, Ella! You're impossible!

Say it in your language …
It's against the rules.
You're impossible!

5 **Look back at the conversation. Complete the sentences.**

1 Can you *give me a hand* with these bags?
2 …. saving this for me until next week?
3 …. lend me some money?

6 **Read the phrases for asking for help. Find three responses in the conversation.**

Asking for help	Responding
Could you … ?	OK.
Can you …?	Sure.
Can/Could you give me a hand with …?	No problem.
Would you mind …-ing …?	Sorry, I can't.

7 **Listen to the conversations. Does each person agree to help or not? Act out the conversations in pairs.**
1.34

Ruby Can you lend me ¹ a pen?
Ella Sorry, I can't. I only have one.

Ash Could you give me a hand with ² this homework?
Ruby Sorry, I can't.

Ella Would you mind ³ carrying my bag?
Tom No problem.

8 **Work in pairs. Replace the words in purple in Exercise 7. Use these words and/or your own ideas. Act out the conversations.**

Can you lend me a calculator?

Sorry, I can't. I only have one.

1 a pencil / a ruler / an eraser

2 my English / these sandwiches / this computer

3 taking a photo / opening the door / coming with me

Grammar • Much, many, a lot of

How much money does she have?	How many T-shirts does she have?
She has a lot of money.	She has a lot of T-shirts.
She doesn't have much/a lot of money.	She doesn't have many/a lot of T-shirts.
She has too much money.	She has too many T-shirts.

Grammar reference page 112

1 **Study the grammar table. Complete the rules with (too) much, (too) many or a lot of.**

1 With countable nouns, we use *a lot of* or …. .
2 With uncountable nouns, we use *a lot of* or …. .
3 In affirmative sentences, we usually use …. .
4 In negative sentences, we can use …. , …. or …. .

2 **Choose the correct options.**

1 There are too *much / many* people here.
2 He doesn't make *much / many* money.
3 She does *a lot of / much* homework every night.
4 How *much / many* credit cards do you have?
5 I ate too *much / many* food yesterday.
6 He took *a lot of / too much* photos.

3 **Complete the text with much, many or a lot of.**

How ¹ *many* underground stores are there in your city or town? In Toronto, Canada, there are 1,200! In the winter there's ² …. snow in Toronto, and people don't spend ³ …. time outside in the cold. In the summer, there are too ⁴ …. cars on the streets and too ⁵ …. pollution. So, instead, ⁶ …. people like shopping on the 28 km of paths under the city.

4 **In pairs, ask and answer about these things.**

cash in your wallet	free time	homework
shoes	T-shirts	

How much free time do you have?

I have a lot of free time.

Reading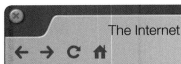

1 Look at the heading and the photos. What connection do you think the photos have to the text?

The Internet

← → C ⌂

The Internet—the World's Biggest Market

1 …. A lot of people find shopping online easier than going to their local mall or to the supermarket, and they love the cheaper prices on the Internet. They also like reading other customers' reviews so they know different people's opinions about a product before they buy it. But for many people, the most important advantage of online shopping is the choice.

2 …. Shopping in your city or town isn't easy if you don't like the same things as everyone else. That isn't a problem online. On the Internet, your shopping mall is the world. You can buy from a Korean music store, a Mexican chili farmer and a Nigerian hat designer all in one afternoon.

3 …. The Internet is also the perfect place to find something strange or unusual. You can buy a jar of Alaskan snow, the poster for a 1920s horror movie or a potato in the shape of a rabbit! Soon after singer Justin Bieber went to the hairstylist, a fan bought a small box of his hair at an auction website for $40,668!

4 …. For some people, experiences are more important than possessions, and they too can find a lot of interesting things on the Internet. Would you like to give your name to a character in a novel or appear in a TV show? Win the right online auction and you can. In 2008, someone even bought an evening with actor Scarlett Johansson for $40,100 (the money went to the charity Oxfam).

You don't get much exercise when you shop online, and you don't see many friendly faces, but if you are looking for something unusual, there's nowhere better!

Key Words

advantage	fan	auction
character	novel	charity

2 Read the text quickly and check your ideas.

3 Read the text again. Match the headings (A–D)
1.35 to the paragraphs (1–4).

A An experience to remember
B International shopping
C Why shop online? *1*
D No one else has that!

4 Read the text again. Answer the questions.

1 How do online shoppers know if other customers like a product? *They read their reviews.*
2 Why is it difficult for some people to find nice things in their city or town?
3 Why did someone pay $40,668 for a box of hair?
4 How, according to the text, can the Internet help you to be on TV?
5 What are the disadvantages of online shopping?

5 In pairs, compare shopping on the Internet with shopping in your local mall.

How much do you buy on the Internet?

I buy about two things online every month.

Listening

1 What problems do people sometimes have when they buy things online? Make a list.

2 Listen to the news report. Was the boy's problem
1.36 one of the things on your list in Exercise 1?

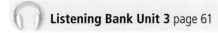

Listening Bank Unit 3 page 61

Writing • A customer review

1 Read the Writing File.

> **Writing File** Expressing opinion
>
> **You can introduce your opinion with:**
>
> I think (that) those boots are a waste of money.
> I don't think (that) it's a very useful bag.
> In my opinion, it's too expensive.
> I find it very difficult to use.

2 Read a customer's online review of a camera. Find three phrases that express an opinion.

Search: digital camera

iPix S70 Blue $150 ☆☆☆☆☆

Other colors available

Your reviews ↘

The iPix S70 camera costs $150 on sale. It comes in a choice of six different colors.
The camera is only 10 cm long and it's very light, so it fits in a small bag easily. It takes great photos inside and outside, and it can make short videos, too. I find it very easy to use.
However, it has some problems. When you take a photo of something too near to the camera, the quality of the photo isn't very good. Another problem is the size of the screen. It isn't big enough if you want to look at your photos on the camera. In my opinion, the iPix S70 isn't the best small camera available. However, for $150, I think it's a good bargain.

3 Complete the sentences with these phrases.

> I don't think ~~I find it~~ I think In my opinion

1 I love this book. *I find it* very interesting.
2 I really don't want that poster. …. that it's very nice.
3 I never go there. …. it's the worst store in town.
4 …. , outdoor markets sell the freshest food.

4 Read the review again and answer the questions.

1 How much does the camera cost?
   It costs $150 on sale.
2 Is there a choice (e.g., of size, color, etc.)?
3 Is its size a good thing or a bad thing? Why?
4 What can you do with it?
5 Is it easy to use?
6 What problems does it have?
7 What is the writer's general opinion of it?

5 You are going to write a customer review of one of these products: a cell phone, an MP3 player or a bag. Use the questions in Exercise 4 to help you. Take notes.

6 Write your customer review. Use "My review" and your notes from Exercise 5.

> **My review**
>
> **Paragraph 1**
> Introduce the product. Say how much it costs and what choices there are (color, size, etc.).
>
> **Paragraph 2**
> Describe the product. Say what you like about it.
>
> **Paragraph 3**
> Describe any problems with the product.
>
> **Paragraph 4**
> Summarize your opinion of the product.

Remember!
- Express opinions with expressions from the Writing File.
- Use the vocabulary and grammar you've practiced in this unit.
- Check your grammar, spelling and punctuation.

Refresh Your Memory!

Grammar • Review

1 Make eight sentences comparing the stores in the table. Use the comparative or superlative form of these adjectives.

> bad   big   cheap   expensive
> ~~friendly~~   good   large   ~~popular~~

	Dollar Stop	Fashionista	Mason's
Size	2,000 m²	900 m²	3,500 m²
Prices	Everything $1	$2–$99	$50–$29,999
Customers per week	5,000	12,000	2,000
Salespeople	unfriendly	very friendly	friendly
Products	not very good	OK	very good

Fashionista is the most popular shop.
Mason's has friendlier salespeople than Dollar Stop.

2 Make sentences.

1 doesn't / She / enough / friends / have
   She doesn't have enough friends.
2 enough / T-shirt / The / big / isn't
3 The / too / expensive / are / scarves
4 is / market / too / The / noisy
5 money / don't / enough / We / earn
6 aren't / enough / My / fashionable / clothes

3 Complete the conversation with *a lot of, much* or *many.*

A I don't have ¹ *many* summer clothes, so I'm going shopping.
B Oh, I need ² .... things downtown. Can I give you a list? I can't go with you because I have too ³ .... homework.
A OK, if you're quick. I don't have ⁴ .... time. There's a bus in five minutes, and you know there aren't ⁵ .... buses on the weekend.
B Thanks. Here's the list. I hope there aren't too ⁶ .... things.
A What? How ⁷ .... hands do you think I have?! I can't carry all this!

Vocabulary • Review

4 Match these words to the definitions (1–5).

> ~~ATM~~   bargain   coin
> customer   sale

1 You use a card to get money from this. *ATM*
2 This type of money is small and hard.
3 When a store has this, the prices are cheaper.
4 This person buys things in stores.
5 This is a product with a cheap price.

5 One of the underlined words in each sentence is incorrect. Correct it.

1 "How much do the jeans <u>~~spend~~</u>?" *cost*
   "Ten dollars. They're a very good <u>price</u>."
2 He <u>wins</u> a lot of money at his market stand because he <u>sells</u> really popular things.
3 Do you want to pay <u>in</u> cash or <u>with</u> credit card?
4 He can't <u>cost</u> designer clothes at the <u>mall</u> in his town.
5 Can I <u>lend</u> a ten-dollar <u>bill</u> so I can buy my train ticket?

Speaking • Review

6 Complete the conversations with these words.
1.37 Then listen and check.

> can   ~~could~~   give   mind
> problem   sorry   sure   with

A ¹ *Could* you lend me your cell phone for a minute, please?
B ² .... . Here you go.

A Would you ³ .... carrying the shopping basket?
B OK. No ⁴ .... .

A ⁵ .... you ⁶ .... me a hand ⁷ .... the food?
B ⁸ .... , I can't. I'm too busy.

Dictation

7 Listen and write in your notebook.
1.38

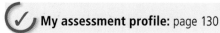
✓ **My assessment profile:** page 130

Math File

Prices of Products Around the World

Do you pay more for products than people in other countries? Look at this table and find out.

	The UK	China	The US	France
ADMIT ONE 54115 54115 Big screen Cinema	£8.00 (€…)	¥30.00 (€…)	$9.00 (€…)	€6.20
	£2.20 (€…)	¥14.50 (€…)	$3.60 (€…)	€3.50
	£3.50 (€…)	¥5.00 (€…)	$3.50 (€…)	€2.40
	£60.00 (€…)	¥388.00 (€…)	$55.00 (€…)	€50.00

Do the math

Do you know how to change one currency into another? Use our easy guide.

First, you must know the exchange rate. Exchange rates change every day. You can find them online or in a newspaper, or in banks and post offices. Then do the math.

> Price in currency A **X**
> Exchange rate for 1 unit of currency A **=**
> Price in currency B

For example:
Price of a burger in South Africa = 17 rand
Exchange rate: 1 rand = 0.10 euros
How much does the burger cost in euros?
17 x 0.10 = 1.70
The burger costs 1.70 euros.

> **Key Words**
> currency   exchange rate

Reading

1 Match the currencies to the countries. What is your country's currency?

> pound (£)   dollar ($)
> euro (€)
> yuan (¥)
> rand (R)

> China
> France
> South Africa
> The UK
> The US

2 Read the magazine article and answer the questions.

1 How much do sneakers cost in the US?
$55.00
2 In which country is a magazine more expensive than a burger?
3 How many magazines can you buy for the price of a movie ticket in China?
4 Name two places where you can find out about exchange rates.

3 Calculate the price in euros of the items from the UK, China and the US in the table in the article. Use the exchange rates below.

exchange rates	
£1	€1.20
¥1	€0.10
US$1	€0.75

4 Listen. Are these statements true (T) or false (F)?
1.39 Use your euro prices from Exercise 3 to help you.

My Math File

5 Find out the price of three items in your country and in two other countries with a different currency. Convert the prices into your currency.

6 Make a poster with the information from Exercise 5. Include a table like the one in the article and sentences comparing the items.

Switzerland has the most expensive coffee. Tickets to soccer games are cheaper in Mexico than in my country.

Review 1

Grammar • Present simple and continuous

1 **Complete the conversation with the Present simple or Present continuous form of the verbs.**

A [1] *Do* you *want* (want) to go out with us tonight? We [2] .... (go) to Pat's house after her music lesson. You know she [3] .... (have) a music lesson at 5 p.m. on Fridays. Then we [4] .... (go) out for pizza at 6 p.m.

B Oh, I [5] .... (play) a tennis match at that time. We always [6] .... (have) matches on Friday nights. But I'm free tomorrow. What [7] .... you .... ? (do)

A Well, I usually [8] .... (go) swimming, but tomorrow I [9] .... (meet) Jane at the café. Why don't you join us?

B Good idea. I [10] .... (go) to the mall anyway, so I can meet you afterward.

• Verb + -ing

2 **Make sentences.**

1 Do / you like / get up / early?
   Do you like getting up early?
2 I / prefer / watch movies to plays.
3 Jenny / hate / do housework.
4 My mom / really enjoy / work in the yard.
5 I / not mind / clean up / my room. But I / hate / iron.

• Past simple

3 **Complete the conversation with the Past simple form of the verbs.**

A What [1] *did* you *do* (do) on the weekend?
B I [2] .... (go) shopping.
A What [3] .... you .... ? (buy)
B I [4] .... (buy) a birthday present for my friend. She [5] .... (have) a party on Saturday night.
A [6] .... (be) it a good party?
B Yes! Her brother's band [7] .... (play), and we all [8] .... (dance). I [9] .... (give) her a CD, and we [10] .... (listen) to that, too.
A What time [11] .... the party .... ? (end)
B I [12] .... (come) home at about 11 p.m. But I think the party [13] .... (end) at midnight!

• Past continuous

4 **Complete the text with the Past continuous forms of the verbs.**

Yesterday, everyone in our house [1] *was doing* (do) something different. My brother and his friends [2] .... (play) soccer in the backyard. My dad [3] .... (fix) his bike. My mom [4] .... (make) a cake and [5] .... (listen) to the radio. And me? I [6] .... (lie) on my bed and [7] .... (read) my favorite magazine! What [8] .... you .... ? (do)

• Past simple vs past continuous

5 **Choose the correct option.**

1 I *was texting / texted* my friend while I *was walking / walked* down the street. Then I *was walking / walked* into a tree!
2 We *were watching / watched* a movie on TV when suddenly it *stopped / was stopping* working. So we *weren't seeing / didn't see* the end of the movie.
3 It *was raining / rained* yesterday, so we *weren't having / didn't have* a picnic.
4 While I *was waiting / waited* at the dentist's, I *was reading / read* magazines.
5 I *was sitting / sat* in a café when I suddenly *was seeing / saw* an old friend.
6 I *was hurting / hurt* my ankle yesterday. I *was standing / stood* on a chair to reach the top shelf when I *was falling / fell*.

• Comparatives and superlatives

6 **Make sentences using the correct form of the adjectives.**

1 A whale / heavy / an elephant.
   A whale is heavier than an elephant.
2 The cheetah is / fast / animal in the world.
3 Which is / big—London or Paris?
4 I think Adam Sandler is / funny / actor in Hollywood.
5 That was / good / pizza / in the world!
6 My math test was / bad / my English test.
7 Tracy lives / far / from school / me.
8 The weather today is / good / yesterday.

• *Too* and *enough*

7 Complete the second sentence so that it means the same as the first. Use the word in parentheses.

1 You aren't old enough to drive. (young)
You are too young to drive.
2 I'm too short to reach that shelf. (tall)
3 You are too sick to go to school today. (well)
4 He isn't strong enough to lift that heavy box. (weak)
5 This T-shirt is too small for me. (big)
6 The tickets are too expensive. (cheap)
7 That theme park ride was boring. It was too slow! (fast)
8 We arrived too late to get the best seats in the theater. (early)

• Much, many, a lot of

8 Complete the sentences with *much, many* or *a lot of*.

1 How *much* do you know about Philadelphia?
2 Do you know, for example, how ....
neighborhoods there are?
3 They're planning to build a new library at our school. There's .... work to do.
4 Let's go somewhere else to eat. There are too .... people at this restaurant.
5 I can't buy that jacket. It costs too .... .
6 Wow! You have so .... DVDs!
7 We don't need any more juice. There's ....
juice left in the bottle.
8 How .... time do we have before class starts?

Speaking • Describing a place

1 Put the conversation in the correct order.

.1. What's your new house like?
.... Yes. There are a lot of flowers and trees in it.
.... Is it big?
.... Is the backyard nice?
.... It's great!
.... Yes. It's bigger than our old house.
When can I come and see it?
Come today, after school!

• Permission

2 Complete the conversation with these words.

| sorry | ~~can~~ | can't | do | mind | OK |

Paul [1] *Can* I go out with Alex tonight, Mom?
Mom No, you [2] .... . You have to do your homework.
Paul Well, is it [3] .... if I go out after that?
Mom Yes, you can. But don't stay out too late.
Paul Er … Alex lives really far away. Do you [4] .... if I stay over at Alex's house tonight?
Mom Yes, I [5] .... ! You can't stay over on a school night.
Paul Well, can you give me a ride home?
Mom No, I'm [6] .... Paul. Maybe you should stay at home after all.

• Asking for help

3 Choose the correct option.

A Could you give me a [1] *hand / lend* with this heavy box, Steve?
B [2] *Sorry. / Sure.*
A Thanks. [3] *Would / Can* you mind [4] *carry / carrying* it to the station for me?
B Sorry, I [5] *don't / can't*. I'm meeting my friend in five minutes and we're going to watch a basketball game.
A Well, could you just carry it to the end of the block?
B [6] *No problem. / Not sure.* You can take a taxi from there.

Vocabulary • Rooms and parts of the house

1 Complete the words for rooms and parts of the house.

1 There is an a *t t i* c at the top of the house.
2 Walk down the s _ _ _ rs to the b _ s _ m _ _t, below the house.
3 We don't have a yard, but we have a small p _ _ _ o.
4 We park the car in the g _ r _ _ e.
5 Our front d _ _ r is red.
6 The rooms have very high c _ _ l _ _ gs.
7 My father works from home. He uses one room as his o _ f _ ce.

• Furniture and household objects

2 Match the words on the left (1–10) to the words on the right (a–j) to make furniture and household objects.

1	alarm	a	case
2	dress	b	chair
3	clos	c	clock
4	arm	d	er
5	cur	e	ions
6	book	f	low
7	cush	g	et
8	pil	h	ror
9	comf	i	tains
10	mir	j	orter

• Adjectives to describe pictures

3 Complete the sentences with these adjectives.

awful	beautiful	blurry	boring
colorful	fake	funny	~~interesting~~
old-fashioned	silly		

1 It doesn't look very *interesting*—it looks pretty boring.
2 The photo isn't very clear. It's .... .
3 The colors are kind of .... . They're just gray and brown.
4 I love this picture—especially the .... red, orange and yellow flowers.
5 This picture makes me laugh. It's very .... .
6 It isn't a modern picture. It's very .... .
7 Is it a real photo, or is it .... ?
8 It isn't serious. It's .... .
9 The picture of the park is ....—it's very pretty.
10 What an ugly place! It looks really .... .

• Adjective + preposition

4 Complete the sentences with the correct preposition.

a If you get bored ¹ *with* the music on your MP3 player, try downloading radio podcasts instead. There are podcasts for all kinds of shows. If you are interested ² .... plays, you can listen to stories or dramas, too. I get tired ³ .... the same old music, so I sometimes listen to an online radio station.
b We're going to a theme park this weekend! I'm really excited ⁴ .... that. I'm not afraid ⁵ .... fast and dangerous rides. I love them!
c I hope I do well on my exams. I want my parents to be proud ⁶ .... me. I don't want them to be angry ⁷ .... me.

• Shopping nouns

5 Complete the sentences with these words.

~~ATM~~	bargains	bill	coins
customers	sale	salesperson	stand

1 You can take money out of an *ATM*.
2 When a store has a .... , things are cheaper, and you can find a lot of .... .
3 A .... works in a store and helps the .... .
4 I have a ten dollar .... and some fifty cents in .... in my pocket.
5 He sells fruits and vegetables at the market. His .... is near the entrance.

• Money verbs

6 Choose the correct option.

The City Market is a very popular market in Kansas City, Missouri. People come there from all over the state to ¹ *buy* / *borrow* things. Most items aren't expensive, so you can find something you can ² *cost* / *afford*. Markets are cheaper than stores in the mall, so you can ³ *save* / *win* some money. But vendors want you to pay ⁴ *in* / *by* cash. They don't have machines for ⁵ *credit* / *spend* cards. If you want to go to the market, I'll ⁶ *borrow* / *lend* you a big shopping bag. You'll need it for all your bargains!

Word list

Unit 1 • Home Sweet Home

Rooms and parts of the house

attic	/ˈæt̬ɪk/
balcony	/ˈbælkəni/
basement	/ˈbeɪsmənt/
ceiling	/ˈsilɪŋ/
driveway	/ˈdraɪvweɪ/
fireplace	/ˈfaɪɚpleɪs/
floor	/flɔr/
garage	/gəˈrɑʒ/
hallway	/ˈhɔlweɪ/
landing	/ˈlændɪŋ/
office	/ˈɔfɪs/
patio	/ˈpæt̬iˌoʊ/
roof	/ruf/
stairs	/stɛrz/
wall	/wɔl/
yard	/yɑrd/

Furniture and household objects

alarm clock	/əˈlɑrm klɑk/
armchair	/ˈɑrmtʃɛr/
blind	/blaɪnd/
bookcase	/ˈbʊk-keɪs/
closet	/ˈklɑzɪt/
comforter	/ˈkʌmfɚt̬ɚ/
curtain	/ˈkɚt̚n/
cushion	/ˈkʊʃən/
dresser	/ˈdrɛsɚ/
mirror	/ˈmɪrɚ/
pillow	/ˈpɪloʊ/
rug	/rʌg/
vase	/veɪs/

Unit 2 • What's the Story?

Adjectives to describe pictures

beautiful	/ˈbyut̬əfəl/
blurry	/ˈblɚi/
boring	/ˈbɔrɪŋ/
colorful	/ˈkʌləfəl/
dark	/dɑrk/
dramatic	/drəˈmæt̬ɪk/
fake	/feɪk/
funny	/ˈfʌni/
horrible	/ˈhɔrəbəl/
interesting	/ˈɪntrɪstɪŋ/

old-fashioned	/ˌoʊld ˈfæʃənd/
silly	/ˈsɪli/

Adjective + preposition

afraid of	/əˈfreɪd əv/
angry with	/ˈæŋgri wɪð, wɪθ/
bad at	/ˈbæd ət/
bored with	/bɔrd wɪð, wɪθ/
excited about	/ɪkˈsaɪt̬ ɪd əˌbaʊt/
good at	/ˈgʊd ət/
interested in	/ˈɪntrɪstɪd ɪn/
popular with	/ˈpɑpyələ wɪð, wɪθ/
proud of	/ˈpraʊd əv/
sorry for	/ˈsɑri fɚ, fɔr/
tired of	/taɪɚd əv/

Unit 3 • It's a Bargain!

Shopping nouns

ATM	/ˌeɪ ti ˈɛm/
bargain	/ˈbɑrgən/
bill	/bɪl/
change	/tʃeɪndʒ/
coin	/kɔɪn/
customer	/ˈkʌstəmɚ/
line	/laɪn/
mall	/mɔl/
market stand	/ˈmɑrkɪt ˌstænd/
price	/praɪs/
products	/ˈprɑdʌkts/
sale	/seɪl/
salesperson	/ˈseɪlzˌpɚsən/
shopping basket	/ˈʃɑpɪŋ ˌbæskɪt/
vendor	/ˈvɛndɚ/

Money verbs

afford	/əˈfɔrd/
borrow	/ˈbɑroʊ/
buy	/baɪ/
cost	/kɔst/
earn	/ɚn/
lend	/lɛnd/
pay by credit card	/ˌpeɪ baɪ ˈkrɛdɪt kɑrd/
pay in cash	/ˌpeɪ ɪn ˈkæʃ/
save	/seɪv/
sell	/sɛl/
spend	/spɛnd/
win	/wɪn/

Vocabulary • News and media

1 Match the pictures (1–4) to three or four of these words and complete the table.
2.1 Then listen, check and repeat.

blog
current affairs show
headline
international news
interview (n, v)
journalist
local news
national news
news anchor
news flash
newspaper
news website
podcast
report (n, v)

2 Complete the sentences with the words in Exercise 1.

1 The *headlines* in today's *newspapers* are all about the football game.
2 I'd love to be a .... on TV or for a newspaper and .... important people.
3 I want to start a .... on the Internet so I can write about my vacations.
4 I often read *Teen News* on my computer. It's a .... for teenagers.
5 I don't usually download .... , but this one is interesting. It's an interview with Justin Bieber.
6 My uncle's a .... . He reads the news on a .... .

3 In pairs, ask and answer.

1 Do you prefer to read the news in a newspaper or online?
2 What was the last news story you read about?
3 Can you name any news anchors?
4 Do you prefer local news or international news?

	1	2	3	4
news anchor	.....			
.....	.....	.....		
.....	.....	.....		
.....				

I prefer reading a newspaper. What about you?

I like reading news online—it's quicker!

Brain Trainer Unit 4
Activity 2
Go to page 60

Reading

1 **You are going to read a survey about teens and the news. Look at the photo and answer the questions.**

1 What is the girl doing?
2 What do you think she is reading about?
3 Do your family or friends read a print newspaper?

2 **Can you predict the results of the survey? Complete the sentences with these numbers.**

| ~~85~~ | 51 | 35 | 31 | 16 | 69 |

85 % of teenagers watch news flashes about important events.
.... % of teenagers watch the news on TV.
.... % log on to news websites.
.... % read the news every day.
.... % watch current affairs shows.
.... % could live without newspapers.

3 **Read the survey quickly and check your answers to Exercise 2.**

4 **Read the survey again. Answer the questions.**

2.2
1 What type of news are teens interested in?
   National news.
2 How many teens think newspapers are important?
3 How did Jake find out about the tsunami in Japan?
4 Why does he like news websites?
5 Why hasn't Lisa read the news this week?
6 Where does she usually read a newspaper?
7 Which stories does she read?

5 **What about you? In pairs, ask and answer the four questions in the survey.**

Survey: Teens and the Media

In last month's issue of *Teen News,* we asked you to mail us your answers to the following questions:

- Have you read or heard today's news headlines?
- Where do you usually get your news from?
- Do you read or listen to the news every day?
- What news are you interested in?

Here are the results!

Most of you (sixty-nine percent) prefer watching the news on TV, and thirty-five percent regularly log on to news websites. Thirty-one percent of you read or listen to the news every day, but only sixteen percent like watching current affairs shows. You're more interested in national news than international news, but nearly eighty-five percent of our readers watch news flashes about important events in the world.

So, is there any room for newspapers in today's world? Twenty-three percent of you said yes, but more than half (fifty-one percent) said you could live without them. Jake and Lisa explain their views:

Jake Moreno (16)
I've never bought a newspaper. I usually find out about the news through a social networking site. That's how I heard about the tsunami in Japan. One of my friends added a link to a news flash. News websites are good too, because you can listen to podcasts and watch videos.

Lisa Sherman (15)
I sometimes look at news websites, but I haven't had time this week (too much homework!). I usually read a newspaper on the school bus. I follow the local news, and I also read the sports section.

Grammar • Present perfect

Affirmative
I/You/We/They have ('ve) read the news.
He/She/It has ('s) read the news.

Negative
I/You/We/They have not (haven't) read the news.
He/She/It has not (hasn't) read the news.

Questions and short answers
Have I/you/we/they heard the news?
Yes, I/you/we/they have. / No, I/you/we/they haven't.
Has he/she/it heard the news?
Yes, he/she/it has. / No, he/she/it hasn't.

Watch Out!
Have you **ever** bought a newspaper?
He has **never** bought a newspaper.

Grammar reference page 114

1 Study the grammar table and Watch Out!
Complete the rules with these words.

> an unspecified past time ever have/has never

1 We use the Present perfect to talk about
an experience that happened at .... , but is
relevant to the present.
2 We make the Present perfect with .... and
the Past participle.
3 We use .... to ask about experiences.
4 We use .... to talk about experiences
we haven't had.

2 Complete the sentences with the Present perfect
form of these verbs.

> buy   ~~not buy~~   not finish
> not go   not hear   write

1 Sorry, I *haven't bought* a newspaper. I haven't
had time!
2 My sister is a journalist. She .... a lot of articles.
3 I can't go out tonight. I .... my homework.
4 He .... finally ... a new cell phone.
5 They .... to the beach. It's too cold!
6 I .... the final score of the game. Did we win?

3 Complete the conversation. Then listen and check.

2.3
Girl ¹ *Have* you *seen* (see) the new school website?
Boy No, I ² .... . Is it good?
Girl It's great! It has school news, movie reviews
and jokes on it.
Boy What about football? ³ .... the PE teacher
.... (write) about our school team's last game?
Girl No, he ⁴ .... . Why don't you write about it?
Boy I don't know how to write a report. ⁵ .... you
.... (ever/do) something like that?
Girl Yes, I ⁶ .... . I ⁷ .... (write) about school
uniforms for the school newspaper before,
and I ⁸ .... (interview) some teachers. You
should interview the principal.
Boy No way! I ⁹ .... (not interview) anyone before!
Girl Well, listen to mine first. They ¹⁰ .... (put)
a podcast of my interviews on the website.

4 Complete the questions and answers.

1 **A** *Have you ever been* (you/ever/be) to the US?
B Yes, I have.
2 **A** .... (you/ever/meet) a famous person?
B No, I .... (never/meet) a famous person.
3 **A** .... (you/ever/play) basketball?
B Yes, I .... .
4 **A** .... (he/ever/write) a blog?
B No, he .... (never/write) a blog.
5 **A** .... (she/ever/be) late for school?
B Yes, she .... !
6 **A** .... (they/ever/buy) a computer game?
B Yes, they .... .

5 What about you? In pairs, ask and answer.

Have you ever …
• go to a rock concert?
• wear red sneakers?
• try skateboarding?
• see a horror movie?
• have a pet?
• write a poem?
• be on TV?
• stand on your head?

> Have you ever been to
> a rock concert?

> Yes, I have. It was fantastic!

Vocabulary • Adverbs of manner

1 Look at these words. Check the meaning in a dictionary. Listen and repeat.

2.4

angrily	badly	carefully	carelessly	early
fast	happily	hard	late	loudly
patiently	quietly	sadly	slowly	~~well~~

Word list page 57
Workbook page 119

2 Complete the sentences with the words in Exercise 1.

1 He's a good journalist. He writes very *well*.
2 She's a hard worker. She works very .... .
3 He felt sad for me. He looked at me .... .
4 They were late for the party. They arrived .... .
5 He's very quiet. He speaks .... , too.
6 The politician was angry. He answered the questions .... .
7 They're slow readers. They read .... .
8 He's so careless. He does things .... .

3 Choose the correct options to complete the text.

How to Be a News Anchor

TV news anchors work very ¹ *hard / badly*. I get up very ² *early / late* every day, around 5 a.m. When I get to the TV studio, there's a lot of information to read. I read it ³ *slowly / fast* so I know the main stories. I read it again later to get more detail. Then a hairstylist does my hair, and I choose my clothes ⁴ *carefully / carelessly*. You can't wear black, white or red—cameras have problems with these colors! I'm always ready early, but I wait ⁵ *angrily / patiently* for the show to start. Then I smile ⁶ *sadly / happily* and read the news headlines. I speak clearly (but not too ⁷ *quietly / loudly*), so people can understand what I say. It's an interesting job, and I do it ⁸ *badly / well*!

4 Correct the sentences. Use these words.

badly	carefully	fast
happily	~~loudly~~	patiently

1 The class sang **quietly**. It was really noisy. *loudly*
2 Jamal spent a long time taking the photo. He did it very **carelessly**.
3 Jasmin smiled **sadly** when she won first prize.
4 We ran very **slowly**. We were late for school!
5 Kevin did **well** on his exams. He didn't get good grades.
6 The teacher explained the homework **angrily**. He wanted everyone to understand.

5 What about you? In pairs, ask and answer.
1 Do you work slowly or fast?
2 Do you get to school early or late?
3 Do you work hard in class?
4 Do you usually play your music loudly or quietly?
5 Do you do usually do well or badly on school exams?

Pronunciation /æ/ and /ɑ/

6a Listen and repeat.

2.5

/æ/	/ɑ/
flash	dark
happily	far
have	hard

b Listen. Copy the table and put these words in the correct column.

2.6

~~album~~	angrily	badly	basket	~~card~~
class	hat	park	party	sadly

/æ/	/ɑ/
album	*card*

c Listen, check and repeat.

2.7

Brain Trainer Unit 4
Activity 3
Go to page 60

Speaking and Listening

1 Look at the photo. Answer the questions.

1 Where are the teenagers?
2 What are they doing?
3 What do you think has happened?

2 Listen and read the conversation.
2.8 Check your answers.

3 Listen and read again. Answer
2.8 the questions.

1 What escaped from the zoo?
   A snake.
2 Where did they find it?
3 Who found it?
4 What did she think it was?
5 What was probably terrified?
6 Who isn't scared of snakes?

4 Act out the conversation in groups of four.

Tom	Hey, have you heard the story about the snake?
Ash	What snake?
Tom	The snake from the zoo. It escaped last week. Well, they have found it.
Ash	Oh yeah? Where?
Tom	In a store in town.
Ash	No! Really?
Tom	Yes, listen to this: "Carrie James, a local teenager, found the snake when she was shopping in Trend clothing store yesterday."
Ella	I don't believe it! I shop there all the time.
Tom	"I thought it was a scarf," said Carrie, "but when I touched it, it moved away quickly."
Ash	That's ridiculous!
Tom	It gets better. "I've never touched a snake before," said Carrie. "I'm glad I didn't try it on!"
Ella	Ugh! Imagine that!
Ruby	Poor snake! It was probably terrified.
Ella	Poor snake? You're kidding!
Ruby	No, I'm not. I really like snakes.

Say it in your language ...
It gets better.
Imagine that!

5 Look back at the conversation. Who says what?

1 No! Really? *Ash*
2 I don't believe it!
3 That's ridiculous!
4 You're kidding!

 6 Read the phrases for expressing doubt and disbelief.

Expressing doubt and disbelief
No! Really?
I don't believe it.
That's strange.
That's impossible.
You're kidding!
That's ridiculous!

 7 Listen to the conversations. Act out the conversations in pairs.
2.9

Ruby	I met ¹ Justin Bieber in LA last week.
Tom	I don't believe it.
Ruby	But it's true!
Ella	² Our school was on TV yesterday.
Ruby	That's impossible!
Ella	No, it isn't. Take a look at ³ the news website.
Tom	I put ⁴ a video of my dog online.
Ash	You're kidding!
Tom	No, I'm not. Here it is.

 8 Work in pairs. Replace the words in purple in Exercise 7. Use these words and/or your own ideas. Act out the conversations.

> I met our principal in the café yesterday.

> I don't believe it.

1 Lady Gaga in New York / Angelina Jolie in Hollywood / LeBron James in Miami

2 my best friend / my dad / my brother

3 the local news / my blog

4 a photo of my party / a video of my cat / a picture of me in my Superman costume

Grammar • Present perfect vs Past simple

Present perfect	Past simple
A snake has escaped from the zoo.	A snake escaped from the zoo last week.
I've never touched a snake before.	She didn't touch the snake.
Have they found the snake?	A teenager found the snake in a store yesterday.

Grammar reference page 114

 1 Study the grammar table. Choose the correct options to complete the rules.

1 We use the *Past simple / Present perfect* to talk about something that happened at an unspecified time in the past, but is relevant to the present.
2 We use the *Past simple / Present perfect* to talk about something that happened at a specific time in the past.

 2 Complete the sentences with the Past simple or Present perfect form of the verbs.

1 **finish**
   a OK, I*'ve finished* my homework. Can I watch TV?
   b I *finished* my homework half an hour ago.
2 **eat**
   a .... you all .... dinner yet?
   b We .... all the pizza last night.
3 **lose**
   a I .... my glasses at the mall last weekend.
   b I .... my glasses again. I really need them!

3 Make conversations.

A you ever / meet a famous person?
   Have you ever met a famous person?
B Yes, I have.
A Really? Who / you / meet?
B I / meet Keira Knightley last year.

A you / ever go / to a skatepark?
B Yes, I have.
A When / you / go?
B I / go / to one last week.

Reading

1 Look at the photo. Answer the questions.

1 What do you think the woman's job is?
2 How would you describe her work?
- dangerous
- safe
- boring
- interesting
- easy
- difficult

Teen News

Profile: Christiane Amanpour

Christiane Amanpour is small with dark hair. She looks like an ordinary person, but she is one of the world's most famous journalists.

Christiane was born in England in 1958 and went to school
5 there and in Iran. She studied journalism in the US, and when she graduated from college, she got a job as an assistant with CNN. "I arrived at CNN with a suitcase, my bicycle and 100 dollars," she says. It was a difficult introduction to journalism, but Christiane worked hard, and she soon
10 became a foreign correspondent.

Life as a foreign correspondent is busy and often dangerous. They fly to different countries and report on international news there. Their reports appear on news websites, in newspapers and on TV, and thousands—
15 sometimes millions—of people see them.

Christiane has been all over the world and reported on many different stories. Some of them are the biggest stories of the twentieth century. She has reported on wars and natural disasters, and she has also interviewed world
20 leaders and politicians. She has often been in danger, but luckily she has never been injured. Christiane won the Courage in Journalism Award in 1994 for her war reports, but she is modest about it. "It's our job to go to these places and bring back stories, just as a window on the
25 world," she says.

Today Christiane anchors an international news show called *Amanpour*. She interviews people in a TV studio, so she doesn't travel much, but she still tells people what is happening in the world. "I believe that good journalism,
30 good television, can make our world a better place," she says.

Key Words	
foreign correspondent	wars
natural disasters	world leaders
politicians	modest

2 Read the magazine article and check your answers to Exercise 1.

3 Read the article again. Answer the questions.

2.10

1 Why is Christiane Amanpour special?
She is one of the world's most famous journalists.
2 Where did she study journalism?
3 What was her first job?
4 What do foreign correspondents do?
5 Why did Christiane win the Courage in Journalism Award?
6 What does she do now?

4 What do these words refer to?

1 there (line 5) *in England*
2 she (line 9)
3 them (line 15)
4 them (line 17)
5 it (line 23)

Listening

1 Look at these opinions about the news. Which do you agree with?
2.11

a I'm not interested in international news.

b The news is usually bad. It's often about wars or natural disasters.

c It's good to know what is happening in the world.

 Listening Bank Unit 4 page 61

2 Think about a story in the news this week. Answer the questions.

1 Is it national, international or local news?
2 Where did you see it?
3 What is the story about?

Writing • A profile

1 Read the Writing File.

> **Writing File** Error correction
>
> When you have finished your writing, always check:
> - spelling
> - punctuation
> - grammar
>
> Then write your final draft.

2 Read the profile. Find and correct six errors.

- two punctuation
- two spelling
- two grammar

1 *canterbury – Canterbury*

> **Profile:** Orlando Bloom

Orlando Bloom is a great actor and is often in the newspapers, but I admire him because of his work for UNICEF *.

Orlando was born in 1977 in a town called canterbury. He has gone to school there with his sister, Samantha. Reading and riting weren't easy for Orlando, but he always wanted to be an actor After school, he studied drama in London, then he got the part of Legolas in *The Lord of the Rings*.

Today Orlando was very famous, but he's used his fame to help other people. He has visited schools and villages in Nepal and has helped to support clean water and education progams there. Orlando Bloom is not just a pretty face, he cares about people and the world around him. That's why I admire him.

* UNICEF is the United Nations children's charity.

3 Look at these sentences about the actor, Orlando Bloom. Find and correct the errors. (S = spelling, G = grammar, P = punctuation)

1 Orlando Bloom is ofen in the newspapers. (S) *often*
2 His most exiting movie is *Pirates of the Caribbean*. (S)
3 When he was 15, he has gotten a tattoo. (G)
4 He broke his nose while he is playing rugby. (G)
5 He has a dog named sidi. (P)
6 Is he working in Hollywood now. (P)

4 Read the profile again. Answer the questions.

1 Who did Orlando go to school with?
   His sister, Samantha
2 What did Orlando always want to be?
3 Where did he study drama?
4 How has he helped other people?
5 Why does the writer admire Orlando Bloom?

5 Think about a famous person who you admire. Answer these questions. Take notes.

1 Why is he/she famous?
2 Why do you admire him/her?
3 When was he/she born?
4 Where did he/she go to school?
5 What does he/she do today?

6 Write a profile of the person you chose in Exercise 5. Use "My famous person" and your notes from Exercise 5.

> **My famous person**
>
> **Paragraph 1**
> Introduction and why you admire him/her
> .... (name) *is a great* .... (job). *I admire him/her because of his/her* .... .
> **Paragraph 2**
> Early life, education and career
> .... *was born in* .... (when?) *in* .... (where?). *After school, he/she* .... (what did he/she do?)
> **Paragraph 3**
> What he/she has done recently and why you admire him/her
> *Today* .... (name) *is* .... (describe him/her). *He/She has* .... (what has he/she done?)

Remember!
- Use the vocabulary from this and earlier units where possible.
- Check your grammar, spelling and punctuation.

Grammar • Review

1 Complete the text about a famous reporter. Use the Present perfect form of the verbs.

Clark Kent works for the *Daily Planet*. He's tired because he ¹ *'s had* (have) a busy day. What ² …. he …. (do)? Well, he ³ …. (meet) the mayor of Metropolis, and he ⁴ …. (write) a report for the newspaper. He ⁵ …. (work) with his friend Lois on a big story. They ⁶ …. (not finish) it because they ⁷ …. (not interview) Lex Luthor. Clark ⁸ …. (not see) Lex today, but he ⁹ …. (fly) around the city and helped people. Clark Kent has two jobs. ¹⁰ …. you …. (ever/ hear) of Superman?

2 Make sentences and questions.

1 you / ever / read / a newspaper on the bus?
   Have you ever read a newspaper on the bus?
2 I / never / play / ice hockey
3 they / ever / watch / a video online?
4 He / never / act / in a movie
5 she / ever / interview / a pop star?
6 We / never / try / playing rugby

3 Choose the correct options.

1 Some teenagers *have never bought* / *never bought* a newspaper.
2 Mike *has read* / *read* an interesting blog about computer games last night.
3 There *has been* / *was* a news flash about a tsunami this morning.
4 She *has never eaten* / *didn't eat* at a pizza place. She doesn't like pizza.
5 We *haven't seen* / *didn't see* the football game last weekend.

Vocabulary • Review

4 Read the definitions and complete the words.

1 You can listen to this on your MP3 player. p_o_dc_a_st
2 This person often writes for a newspaper. j_ _rn_l_st
3 The most important news stories are the h_ _dl_n_s.
4 Important new stories usually appear in a n_ws fl_sh on TV.
5 People use this to write about their everyday lives. bl_g
6 On a computer, we can read the news on a n_ws w_bs_t_.

5 Complete the sentences with the correct adverb form of the adjective in parentheses.

1 The actor is smiling *happily* (happy) in the photo.
2 My brother is playing his music very …. (loud).
3 Saul always does his homework very …. (careful).
4 I play tennis really …. (bad).
5 The reporter waited …. (patient) for his first interview to begin.
6 The bus doesn't go very …. (fast), but it's cheaper than the train.

Speaking • Review

6 Complete the conversation with these words. Then listen and check.
2.12

| happen   headlines   ~~heard~~   impossible   kidding |

Girl Have you ¹ *heard* the news? An elephant has escaped from the zoo.
Boy That's ² …. !
Girl No, it isn't. Look at the ³ …. . I'm not ⁴ …. .
Boy Wow! It *is* true. That's ridiculous!
Girl I know, but how did it ⁵ …. ?

Dictation

7 Listen and write in your notebook.
2.13

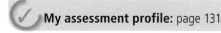
✓ **My assessment profile:** page 131

Tavi Gevinson's Profile

Age	Home country
14 years old	United States

My favorite things …

fashion, writing (check out my fashion blog and Internet magazine for teenage girls), art

Reading

1 Read Tavi's profile. Are the statements true (T) or false (F)?

1 Tavi is from the US. *T*
2 She likes sports.
3 She has an online magazine.
4 The magazine is for adult women.

2 Read the article. Answer the questions.

2.14
1 How old was Tavi when she started her fashion blog?
She was eleven.
2 What did Tavi start at age sixteen?
3 How often is Tavi's online magazine updated?
4 What topics does the magazine cover?
5 What makes Tavi different from other teenagers?

Tavi Gevinson: Writer and Magazine Editor

Tavi Gevinson was born in 1996. She has two older sisters and lives with her family in Oak Park, Illinois. She just graduated from high school and is planning to go to college.

When Tavi was a child, she became interested in fashion and art, and began to explore fashion blogs and magazines. She wanted to present her personal style to other people and talk about trends in fashion. So she started writing her own blog when she was only eleven years old. The blog became popular very fast, and Tavi attended New York Fashion Week and gave interviews in several magazines.

At the age of sixteen, Tavi started her second website, *Rookie*, which is an online magazine for teenage girls (www.rookiemag.com). She explains, "I just felt like there wasn't really anything … that was honest … to an audience of teenage girls or respected their intelligence." The online magazine helps teenage girls to connect with each other and share their experiences. It covers a different theme each month, like "The Great Unknown" or "Together," and is updated three times a day. Many teenage girls contribute their writing, photographs, illustrations or videos to the website. The magazine talks about different cultural and political topics that are important to teenagers today. Tavi works as the magazine's editor-in-chief, and she has edited print versions of the best content from the website, called *Rookie Yearbook*.

Tavi is much busier than most teenagers. She works very hard on her magazine and travels a lot. But she is happy to be part of *Rookie*. "It's a job. … And I'm OK with that, 'cause it's something that I care about," she says.

Key Words

magazine	contribute	theme
editor	connect	content

Class discussion

1 Do you read any blogs on the Internet? What are they about?
2 Would you write about your personal life online? Why?/Why not?
3 Do you feel that the Internet connects teenagers or makes them more lonely?

Grammar • Present perfect

1 Complete the sentences with the Present perfect form of the verbs.

1 *Have* you *ever been* (be) to Russia?
2 No. But I .... (always want) to go there.
3 I .... (never try) Japanese food.
4 Kelly .... (not finish) her project.
5 My brother .... (always want) to be a pilot.
6 The students .... (not do) their homework again.
7 Where .... you .... (be)? I .... (not see) you for a long time.

• Present perfect vs Past simple

2 Complete the conversations with the Present perfect or Past simple form of the verbs.

A ¹ *Have* you *ever ridden* (ride) a camel?
B Yes, I ² .... (ride) one. I ³ .... (take) a trip through the desert in Morocco once.
A When ⁴ .... you .... (go) to Morocco?
B We ⁵ .... (spend) a week there last year.
A When ⁶ .... you .... (come) back from vacation?
B I ⁷ .... (fly) back last night.
A What ⁸ .... (be) it like?
B Great! ⁹ .... you .... (ever go) to Florida?
A No, I ¹⁰ .... (not).

• Present perfect + *for* and *since; How long?*

3 Make sentences with *How long?* Complete the answers with *for* or *since*.

1 **A** you / live / in this house?
   How long have you lived in this house?
2 **B** .... I was a child—so, ... fifteen years!
3 **A** your father / work / in the bank?
4 **B** .... five years.
5 **A** you have / the same hairstyle?
6 **B** .... I was about six!
7 **A** you know / your best friend?
8 **B** .... three years.
9 **A** your class / study / English?
10 **B** .... we were in elementary school.

• Past simple with *just*

4 Complete the sentences with *just* and the Past simple.

1 **A** Something smells delicious in your kitchen. *Did you just bake* a cake? (bake)
2 **B** Yes! I .... it out of the oven. (take)
3 I'm really tired. I .... for a run around the park. (go)
4 Stella .... back from vacation. (arrive)
5 I .... my math homework—after two hours! (finish)
6 I'm crying, because I .... a sad movie on TV. (watch)

• Have to/Don't have to

5 Rewrite the sentences using the correct form of *have to* or *don't have to*.

1 It's essential to wear a helmet on a bike. *You have to wear* a helmet.
2 It's not essential to book tickets in advance. You .... tickets in advance.
3 Swimmers need swimming caps. It's a rule. Swimmers .... wear swimming caps.
4 You can sit down if you are tired. You .... stand.
5 You aren't allowed to arrive late. You .... on time.
6 You can have lunch at school or at home. It's your choice. You .... have lunch at school.

• Must/Mustn't

6 Make rules with *must* or *mustn't* for these signs.

You mustn't park here.

• Predictions with *will*, *won't*, *might*

7 **Choose the correct option.**

1 Look at those dark storm clouds. It *won't* / *will* rain later.
2 I'm not sure if I'm going to Mark's party. I *will* / *might* go.
3 They've been together for a really long time. I'm sure they *might* / *will* get married.
4 This answer *might* / *will* be right. I'm not sure.
5 I promise—I *might not* / *won't* tell anyone your secret.

Speaking • Doubt and disbelief

1 **Complete the conversation with these words.**

believe	impossible	~~kidding~~	Really

A Have you heard about this amazing coincidence? A man was walking under a window at the top of a building when a baby fell.
B You're ¹ *kidding*!
A No, it's true. And he was passing at just the right time, so he caught the baby in his arms!
B No! ² .... ?
A Yes, I read it in the paper. And then the same thing happened a few years later.
B I don't ³ .... it.
A It happened to the same man, outside the same building!
B That's ⁴ .... !
A I know, it's the strangest thing.

• Asking for information

2 **Put the conversation in the correct order.**

_1._ Excuse me, can you help me? I'm looking for the museum. Do you know where it is?
.... It's a nice walk from here, or you can take a bus.
.... Yes, I do. It's just across the river, on the left.
.... Oh yes, there are a lot of restaurants there.
.... I'd like to walk. But is it far?
.... OK, so we have to cross the river. How can we get to the river?
.... That doesn't sound too far. And are there any good places to eat near there?
.... No, it's about a twenty-minute walk.

• Giving advice

3 **Complete the conversation with these phrases.**

I don't think you should worry	Maybe you should tell
~~Why don't you talk~~	You shouldn't pretend

A What's wrong? You look really upset.
B I feel awful about my science exam results. I don't know how I'm going to tell my parents I did so badly. But I'm really bad at science, and I want to study drama instead.
A ¹ *Why don't you talk* to your parents about it?
B The trouble is, they think I really like science.
A ² .... them the truth.
B They'll be upset. After all, they're both doctors.
A ³ .... about that. They'll understand. ⁴ .... you're interested in something when you aren't.
B Yes, maybe you're right.

Vocabulary • News and media

1 **Match the phrases (1–8) to their definitions (a–h).**

1 an online diary *h*
2 the title of a newspaper article
3 a formal question-and-answer session with a person
4 a sudden news announcement
5 a person who writes newspaper articles
6 a newspaper article
7 a person who gives the news on TV
8 a news show that can be downloaded on an MP3 player

a interview
b journalist
c headline
d news flash
e news anchor
f podcast
g report
h blog

• Adverbs of manner

2 Complete the sentences with these adverbs.

angrily	carefully	early	fast
late	loudly	~~quietly~~	sadly

1 Please enter the room *quietly*—students are taking exams.
2 Can you speak more .... ? I can't hear you— it's very noisy in here.
3 Please drive ....—the roads are dangerous.
4 He's a fantastic athlete. He can run so .... .
5 "Go away," he said, quietly but .... .
6 I thought it would be a funny movie, but it ended so .... I cried.
7 If you don't get up soon, you'll arrive at school .... for your classes.
8 It's best to arrive ....—then we'll get the best seats in the theater.

• Vacation

3 Match the verbs (1–8) to the words (a–h) to make vacation phrases.

1 book		a	a travel blog
2 eat		b	camping
3 go		c	in a hotel
4 pack		d	a flight
5 stay		e	a tent
6 get		f	a tan
7 put up		g	your bag
8 write		h	out

• Meanings of *get*

4 Replace *get* using a different verb with the same meaning.

1 When my parents <u>get</u> old, I'll take care of them.
   When my parents become old, I'll take care of them.
2 Can you <u>get</u> some milk when you go to the store?
3 What time will we <u>get</u> home?
4 Did you <u>get</u> an email from Laura about her party?
5 <u>Get</u> off the bus when you see a big gray building in front of you.
6 The dog ran very fast to <u>get</u> the ball.

• Household chores

5 Match the verbs (1–8) to the words (a–h) to make household chores.

1 clear		a	the floor
2 do		b	your bed
3 make		c	the dog
4 load		d	the table
5 mow		e	the trash
6 sweep		f	the lawn
7 take out		g	the ironing
8 walk		h	the dishwasher

• Feelings adjectives

6 Complete the sentences with these adjectives.

confident	confused	disappointed	glad
grateful	~~jealous~~	nervous	upset

1 Don't be *jealous* of people who seem to have more than you do.
2 My exam is tomorrow, but I'm not .... . I worked hard, so I'm .... I'll do well.
3 Could you explain that to me again? I'm .... .
4 Thank you very much. I'm very .... for your help.
5 Carla's .... because her cat died.
6 I'm so .... you're back! I missed you.
7 I'm .... that I didn't get the job.

Word list

Unit 4 • In the News

News and media

blog	/blɑg/
current affairs show	/ˈkʌrənt əˈfɛrz ʃoʊ/
headline	/ˈhɛdlaɪn/
international news	/ˌɪntəˈnæʃənəl ˈnuz/
interview (n, v)	/ˈɪntəˌvyu/
journalist	/ˈdʒɚnl-ɪst/
local news	/ˌloʊkəl ˈnuz/
national news	/ˌnæʃənl ˈnuz/
news anchor	/ˈnuz ˌæŋkɚ/
news flash	/ˈnuz flæʃ/
newspaper	/ˈnuzˌpeɪpɚ/
news website	/ˈnuz ˌwɛbsaɪt/
podcast	/ˈpɑdkæst/
report (n, v)	/rɪˈpɔrt/

Adverbs of manner

angrily	/ˈæŋgrəli/
badly	/ˈbædli/
carefully	/ˈkɛrfəli/
carelessly	/ˈkɛrlɪsli/
early	/ˈɚli/
fast	/fæst/
happily	/ˈhæpəli/
hard	/hɑrd/
late	/leɪt/
loudly	/ˈlaʊdli/
patiently	/ˈpeɪʃəntli/
quietly	/ˈkwaɪətli/
sadly	/ˈsædli/
slowly	/ˈsloʊli/
well	/wɛl/

Unit 5 • Enjoy Your Vacation!

Vacation

book a flight	/ˌbʊk ə ˈflaɪt/
book a hotel	/ˌbʊk ə hoʊˈtɛl/
buy souvenirs	/baɪ ˌsuvəˈnɪr, ˈsuvəˌnɪr/
check into a hotel	/ˌtʃɛk ɪntʊ ə hoʊˈtɛl/
eat out	/ˌit ˈaʊt/
get a tan	/gɛt ə ˈtæn/
get lost	/gɛt ˈlɔst/
go camping	/ˌgoʊ ˈkæmpɪŋ/
go sightseeing	/ˌgoʊ ˈsaɪtˌsiɪŋ/
lose your luggage	/ˌluz yɚ ˈlʌgɪdʒ/
pack your bag	/ˌpæk yɚ ˈbæg/
put up a tent	/ˌpʊt ʌp ə tɛnt/
stay in a hotel	/ˌsteɪ ɪn ə hoʊˈtel/
take a trip	/ˌteɪk ə ˈtrɪp/
write a travel blog	/ˌraɪt ə ˈtrævəl blɒg/

Meanings of get

arrive	/əˈraɪv/
become	/bɪˈkʌm/
bring	/brɪŋ/
buy	/baɪ/
move	/muːv/
receive	/rɪˈsiːv/
walk	/wɔːk/

Unit 6 • That's Life!

Household chores

clear the table	/ˌklɪr ðə ˈteɪbəl/
cook a meal	/ˌkʊk ə ˈmil/
do the dishes	/ˌdu ðə ˈdɪʃɪz/
do the ironing	/ˌdu ðɪ ˈaɪɚnɪŋ/
do the laundry	/ˌdu ðə ˈlɔndri/
feed the cat	/ˌfid ðə ˈkæt/
hang out the laundry	/ˌhæŋ aʊt ðə ˈlɔndri/
load the dishwasher	/ˌloʊd ðə ˈdɪʃˌwɑʃɚ/
make your bed	/ˌmeɪk yɚ ˈbɛd/
mow the lawn	/ˌmoʊ ðə ˈlɔn/
set the table	/ˌsɛt ðə ˈteɪbəl/
sweep the floor	/ˌswip ðə ˈflɔr/
take out the trash	/ˌteɪk aʊt ðə ˈtræʃ/
vacuum the floor	/ˈvækyum ðə ˈflɔr/
walk the dog	/ˌwɔk ðə ˈdɔg/
wash the car	/ˌwaʃ ðə ˈkɑr/

Feelings adjectives

confident	/ˈkɑnfədənt/
confused	/kənˈfyuzd/
disappointed	/ˌdɪsəˈpɔɪntɪd/
embarrassed	/ɪmˈbærəst/
fed up	/ˌfɛd ˈʌp/
glad	/glæd/
grateful	/ˈgreɪtfəl/
guilty	/ˈgɪlti/
jealous	/ˈdʒɛləs/
lonely	/ˈloʊnli/
nervous	/ˈnɚvəs/
relaxed	/rɪˈlækst/
relieved	/rɪˈlivd/
upset	/ˌʌpˈsɛt/

Brain Trainers

Unit 1
Find the difference

1. Look at the photo on page 14 for one minute. Now study this photo. What differences can you find?

Vocabulary

2a. Find the word that doesn't belong in each box. You have one minute.

> wall   roof   ceiling
> garage   floor

> attic   stairs
> hallway   basement   office

> landing   yard   balcony
> patio   driveway

2b. Arrange the letters in bold to make a new home word.

3. Look at the objects in the grid for one minute. Cover the grid and write the words in your notebook. How many objects can you remember?

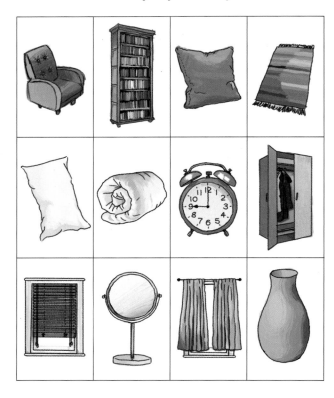

Unit 2
Find the difference

1. Look at the photo on page 24 for one minute. Now study this photo. What differences can you find?

Brain Trainers

Vocabulary

2 Make words. Each word has three shapes.

inte-rest-ing

col rest ful

hor ma ble

3 Work in pairs. Say an adjective. Your partner says the adjective and correct preposition. Then switch roles.

proud	angry	bad	tired
excited	bored	sorry	interested
good	afraid	popular	

> proud

> proud of

Unit 3

Find the difference

1 Look at the photo on page 34 for one minute. Now study this photo. What differences can you find?

Vocabulary

2 Work in pairs. Student A chooses a shopping word. Student B asks Student A the questions below. Student B guesses the word.

coin
bargain   salesperson
line
price   change   product
vendor   customers

Questions
How many syllables are there?
How many letters are there?
How many vowels are there?

> How many letters are there?

> Seven.

3a Complete the five pairs of money verbs below. You have one minute.

b_y   s_ _l
s_ v_   sp_ _d
w_n   e_ _n
c_ s_   _ff_ _ d
l_ _ d   b_ _ r_ w

3b Complete the sentence with two money phrases.

You can pay for things in c_ _h or by c_ _ _ _ t
c _ _ _ .

Brain Trainers

Unit 4
Find the difference

1. Look at the photo on page 48 for one minute. Now study this photo. What differences can you find?

Vocabulary

2. How many *news* words can you think of in one minute? Try to remember at least seven.

    1 *local news*

3a. Read the pairs of words aloud three times. Cover them and read the list below. Which word is missing?

quietly → loudly   carefully → carelessly

happily → sadly   patiently → angrily

| carefully | angrily | loudly | happily |
| quietly | patiently | carelessly | |

3b. Now make more adverbs using the different colored letters. Then match the opposites.

well – badly

Unit 5
Find the difference

1. Look at the photo on page 58 for one minute. Now study this photo. What differences can you find?

Vocabulary

2. Look at the pictures for two minutes. Try to remember them in order. Then cover them. Take turns making suggestions. Can you remember all nine?

Listening Bank

Unit 1

1 Listen again. Listen to the description of Hannah's
1.11 room and what that says about her personality.

pale walls – talkative

2 Listen again. Complete the sentences.
1.11
1 Hannah's walls are pale *yellow*.
2 There's a bright green .... on the bed.
3 She .... trying new things.
4 She has pictures of .... and friends on the walls.
5 Her room is pretty .... at the moment.
6 Her .... likes cleaning up in her room.

Unit 2

1 Listen again. Choose the correct option.
1.24
1 The picture is *real* / *fake*.
2 The men were *240* / *3,300* meters above
the streets.
3 The men were working in *Slovakia* / *America*.
4 Gusti Popovic is the man *on the right* / *on the left*.
5 He sent *a letter* / *a postcard* with the photo.
6 Gusti Popovic was *good at* / *bad at* his job.

2 Listen again. Answer the questions.
1.24
1 Does the boy think the photo is real at first?
No, he doesn't.
2 What does the girl say about Charles Ebbets?
3 What does the boy ask about the men?
4 How does the girl identify Gusti Popovic?
5 Does she say he sent his wife a photo?

Unit 3

1 Listen again. What do these numbers refer to?
1.36
1 16 *the age of the boy*
2 $95
3 2
4 20
5 65,000

2 Listen again and complete the sentences.
1.36
1 The boy bought a *console* and two games online.
2 The console arrived in the .... .
3 There were a lot of 20-dollar .... in the box.
4 The boy and his parents talked to the .... .
5 They were worried the money came from .... .
6 The police want to find the owner of the .... .

Unit 4

1 Listen. Match the speakers (1–3) to the opinions
2.11 (a–c).

Speaker 1
Speaker 2
Speaker 3
a I'm not interested in international news.
  It's not important to me.
b The news is always bad. It's about wars or
  natural disasters.
c It's good to know what's happening in the world.

2 Listen again. Choose the correct options.
2.11
1 Speaker 1 *has read* / *hasn't read* the news today.
2 He *sometimes* / *often* reads his dad's newspaper.
3 He *has* / *doesn't have* time to read the
  newspaper every day.
4 Speaker 2 listened to the news *on the radio* / *on TV*.
5 She thinks there was a headline about
  a *politicians* / *world leaders* meeting.
6 She *can* / *can't* remember all of today's headlines.
7 Speaker 3 read the headlines *in a newspaper* /
  on a news website.
8 The Yankees are playing the Red Sox next
  month / *week*.
9 Speaker 3 is interested in *the sports section* /
  general news.

Reading

1 Read about Homes in the US. Why are detached 3.41 houses often located in the suburbs?

2 Read about Homes in the US again. Are the statements true (T) or false (F)? Correct the false statements.

1 Row houses usually have a big yard.
2 Sixty-four percent of homes in the US are detached houses.
3 There are more homes in large apartment buildings than there are mobile homes in the US.
4 There are a lot of large apartment buildings in cities.

Your Culture

3 In pairs, answer the questions.

1 In your area, what type of home do most people live in?
2 Which of these things are common in homes in your area?
  • an attic   • a balcony   • a basement
  • a garage   • a yard
3 Think of another part of your country. What types of homes are popular there?
4 Are there many very tall buildings in big cities? Are they homes, offices or both?

4 Write a short paragraph about homes in your country. Use your answers to Exercise 3 and the Homes in the US examples to help you.

Types of Homes in the US

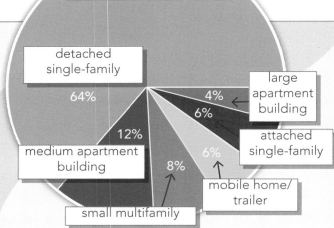

detached single-family — 64%
large apartment building — 4%
attached single-family — 6%
medium apartment building — 12%
mobile home/trailer — 6%
small multifamily — 8%

Detached single-family houses
Detached single-family houses are separate buildings usually surrounded by a yard. They are the most common type of house in the US. Single-family homes often include a garage. They come in a few different architectural styles, depending on the region of the country. They are often located in American suburbs, where larger lots of land and fewer people per square kilometer allow for this type of house.

Row houses
There are a few different types of attached single-family houses in the US: row houses, townhomes and duplexes are the primary types. They share at least one wall and are often found in semiurban or urban areas. They often include a patio or small yard in the back, and sometimes have a garage or driveway for parking.

Small/medium multifamily houses
One-fifth of the housing units in the US are small (2–4 units) to medium (5–49 units) multifamily buildings or apartment buildings and complexes. Each unit could be as small as a studio apartment or could include three to four bedrooms.

Large apartment buildings
Large apartment buildings with more than 50 units are more common in US cities. Some apartments have balconies, and buildings often include one or more shared facilities.

Mobile homes or trailers
Mobile homes are an inexpensive form of housing in the US. People often rent a small space in an area of land, called a trailer park, to set up their mobile home and connect it to city facilities, like water and sewer.

Reading

1 Read about the Republic of Ireland. Which of
3.42 these things are mentioned?

business	dancing	mountains	religion
technology	tradition	TV	

2 Read about the Republic of Ireland again and choose the correct options.

1 *All / Some* of Ireland is in the United Kingdom.
2 Irish is the main language in *some / all* schools in Ireland.
3 In Irish dancing, you move your *feet / arms*.
4 Some people say that *not many / many* Irish people talk a lot.

3 In pairs, answer the questions.

1 Was your country ever ruled by another country? Which one? Did this change your language or other parts of your culture?
2 What type of dancing is your country famous for? Have you ever tried it?
3 Is there anywhere in your country that has a strange tradition? What is it?

4 Write a short paragraph about your country. Use your answers to Exercise 3 and the Republic of Ireland examples to help you.

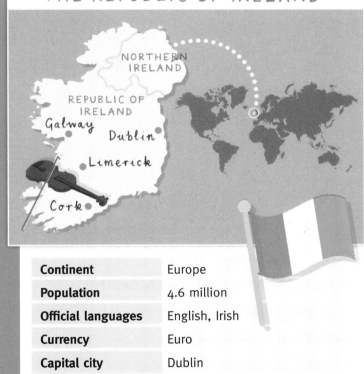

THE REPUBLIC OF IRELAND

Continent	Europe
Population	4.6 million
Official languages	English, Irish
Currency	Euro
Capital city	Dublin

North and South

For many centuries Ireland was ruled by the English, but in the early twentieth century, most of the island became an independent country, the Republic of Ireland. Northern Ireland, however, continued to be part of the United Kingdom. The two parts of Ireland have a shared culture, but there are some religious differences. In the north, most people are Protestants; in the south, most people are Catholics.

This is a shamrock, the symbol of Ireland

Language

Only about one percent of the population now speaks Irish as their main language at home. Most people speak English. However, more and more children are going to Irish-speaking schools, and there are several Irish TV channels, radio stations and newspapers.

Culture

Ireland has a strong cultural influence on the English-speaking world. It has produced many great writers, including Oscar Wilde and George Bernard Shaw; actors, including Pierce Brosnan and Colin Farrell; and musicians, including U2. Irish step dancing—fast foot movements while the body and arms don't move—has also become popular around the world.

The Gift of Gab

At Blarney Castle in the south of Ireland, you can find the Blarney Stone. According to tradition, if you kiss this special stone you will have the "gift of gab"—the ability to talk well and persuade people easily. Some people think that the Irish are the most talkative people in the world. Have they all kissed the Blarney Stone?

Reading

(1) **Read about Sports in the UK.**
3.43 **Which sport**

1 is the UK's favorite?
2 is popular in the summer?
3 is popular with older people?
4 shares its name with a school?

(2) **Read about Sports in the UK again. Answer the questions.**

1 How long are the longest cricket games?
2 In soccer, what important things happened in the UK before they happened in other countries?
3 What three differences are there between soccer and rugby?
4 Why did the king make playing golf illegal?

Your Culture

(3) **In pairs, answer the questions.**

1 Are any of the sports on this page popular in your country? Which ones? Are you a fan of these sports?
2 What sports started in your country? Do you like playing or watching them?
3 What are the most important sports events in your country? Where and when do they happen?

(4) **Write a short paragraph about sports in your country. Use your answers to Exercise 3 and the Sports in the UK examples to help you.**

SPORTS in the UK

Cricket

Cricket began in England about four hundred years ago. Today, there are cricket games all over the country on summer weekends. A local game takes all afternoon.

Professional games at famous stadiums, like Lord's in London, can last for five days, and there is often no winner at the end. People play cricket in most English-speaking countries, and it is very popular in India and Pakistan.

Soccer

The UK was the first country in the world with international soccer teams, professional players and a national soccer tournament. Today soccer is the UK's most

popular sport, and the English Premier League has some of the world's most famous clubs and players. The most important game of the year is the FA Cup Final at London's Wembley Stadium.

Rugby

This sport began in Rugby School, a famous English school. It is like soccer, but there are some big differences. The ball is an oval shape, and you can carry it as

well as kick it. You can also pull players off their feet. Every year there is an important tournament, the Six Nations, between the teams of England, Scotland, Wales, Ireland, France and Italy.

Golf

Golf began in Scotland. In the fifteenth century, the sport was illegal— the king was worried that it was taking too much of people's time. Later, the sport became

popular around the world. Many older people play golf in the UK today, and some of the best professional players are British.

MOVE IT!

WORKBOOK WITH MP3S

SPLIT EDITION

3A

JOE MCKENNA

SERIES CONSULTANT: CARA NORRIS-RAMIREZ

Contents

Starter Unit

Grammar and Vocabulary • To be

1 Complete the conversations with the correct form of *to be*.

1 **A** *Is* Emma your sister?
  B No, she *isn't*.
2 **A** Where .... you from?
  B I .... from Sweden.
3 **A** How old .... your parents?
  B Dad .... 38 and Mom .... 34.

• Have

2 Match the questions (1–4) to the answers (a–d). Then complete the answers with the correct form of *have*.

1 Do you have any pets?   *d*
2 Do your parents have a car?
3 Does Bethany have red hair?
4 Do we have time for a sandwich?

a No, she doesn't. She .... brown hair.
b Yes, we do. We .... class in fifteen minutes.
c Yes, they do. They .... a big family car.
d No, I don't. I don't *have* any animals.

• *Be* and *have*

3 Choose the correct options.

1 Tamara (is)/ *has* 16 years old.
2 My cousins *are* / *have* a big house.
3 Sorry, I *'m not* / *don't have* time to talk right now.
4 Sara's boyfriend *is* / *has* very tall.
5 Kevin *is* / *has* long brown hair.
6 My grandparents *are* / *have* very active.

• Possessive *'s*

4 Look at the picture and complete the sentences with *'s* or *s'*.

We're the Russell family. Our parents, Cathy and Matt, have three children. The [1] children*'s* names are Ben, Laura and Phil. (That's me, Laura, in the middle!) That's [2] Mom .... car, and you can also see [3] Dad .... bicycle. We have three dogs. The [4] dog .... names are Fido, Blackie and Moonie. That's our [5] family .... house behind them. We live at number 34, and our neighbors, the Watsons, live at number 36. Our dogs often run after the [6] Watson .... cat. Their [7] cat .... name is Smoky.

• *Is* and possessive *'s*

5 Read the conversation. Look at the *'s*. Write *is* or *possessive*.

A What**'s** your last name?   [1] *is*
B It**'s** Kennedy. [2] ....
A My aunt**'s** name**'s** Kennedy, too! Where**'s** the name from? [3] ....
  [4] .... [5] ....
B My father says it**'s** from Ireland.
  [6] ....

• Subject and object pronouns

6 **Complete the sentences with the correct pronouns.**

1 I'm going shopping. Do *you* want to come with *me*?
2 Stella's upstairs. .... 'll be down in a minute, and then you can talk to ....
3 Tom's working. .... 'll come home at two o'clock, and .... 'll have lunch together.
4 Are the children outside? Can you ask .... to come inside? .... need to take a bath.
5 We got a letter from Brian! .... always writes to .... in the summer.

• Possessive adjectives

7 **Complete the sentences with the correct possessive adjectives.**

1 We're from Japan. *Our* names are Yumi and Keiko.
2 He's the manager. .... car's parked at the front door.
3 I'm the new teacher. It's .... job to help you speak English.
4 That's Barry's bike. .... frame is made of aluminum.
5 She's a cyclist. .... name's Yadida.

• Common verbs

8 **Put the letters in the correct order to complete the text.**

Today we're reporting from our summer camp. There are a lot of activities here for teenagers. We can ¹ *climb* (mcibl) a wooden tower,
² .... (upmj) into the pool and then
³ .... (msiw) to the side. We can
⁴ .... (lyf) a kite, or we can
⁵ .... (lisa) in a small boat on the lake.
Then, if we're not too tired, we can
⁶ .... (nur) around the lake or
⁷ .... (lypa) tennis with a friend. At the end of the day, there's always a good meal, where we can ⁸ .... (tea) as much as we like!

• Prepositions

9 **Look at the picture. Correct the prepositions in the sentences.**

up
1 There are two people walking ~~down~~ the hill.

2 A man is fishing behind the bridge.

3 Two people are walking under the bridge.

4 There's a wall behind the parking lot.

5 There's a boy standing on top of the wall.

6 There's a man reading on the trees.

Indefinite pronouns

10 Complete the conversations with these words.

~~anyone~~	anything	Everyone	everything
no one	someone	Something	

1 **A** Hello! Is *anyone* home?
  B There's no noise! Can you hear the TV
    or .... ?
  A No. It looks like there's .... in
    the house.
2 **A** The town is very quiet today!
  B Yes! .... is at home watching
    the football game.
  A Well, I need .... to take me
    to the station!
3 **A** Is .... OK?
  B No. .... is wrong with my leg.

Everyday objects

11 Match these words to the definitions (1–6).

sweater	magazine	notebook
poster	wallet	~~watch~~

1 We use this to tell time.   *watch*
2 This is like a really big photo. We often put
  it on the wall.   ....
3 A book for writing in.   ....
4 We keep our money in one of these.
  ....
5 We often read one in the dentist's
  waiting room.   ....
6 This is a warm top.   ....

School subjects

**12 Match the school subjects (1–8) to the related
words (a–h).**

1 art	a kings, queens and wars
2 English	b guitars and drums
3 geography	c laboratory, experiments
4 history	d algebra, geometry
5 literature	e grammar, vocabulary
6 math	f Picasso and Van Gogh
7 music	g novels, plays and poems
8 science	h countries, mountains

Present simple: affirmative and negative

13 Make sentences in the Present simple.

1 On weekends I / not get up / before ten o'clock
  On weekends, I don't get up before ten o'clock.
2 We / have lunch / at two o'clock
  ....
3 Tina / play / volleyball on Saturdays
  ....
4 Tony never / arrive / on time
  ....

Present simple: questions and short answers

**14 Complete the questions with these words.
Then write the correct verb in the answers.**

Does	drive	~~have~~	like

1 Do we *have* any homework for tomorrow?
  Yes, we *do*.
2 .... Lucas work on the weekend?
  No, he ....
3 Do you .... living in the city?
  Yes, I ....
4 Do your parents .... to work?
  No, they ....

Adverbs of frequency

**15 Rewrite the sentences. Put the adverbs of
frequency in the correct place.**

1 Sophie remembers phone numbers! (never)
  Sophie never remembers phone numbers!
2 Jo and Ian don't play tennis on Fridays. (usually)
  ....
3 I go to the movies. (hardly ever)
  ....
4 Susan orders chicken at the restaurant. (always)
  ....
5 We don't have time to watch TV. (often)
  ....
6 Ana and her friends go horseback riding.
  (sometimes)
  ....

Numbers and dates

16 **Write the numbers and dates in words.**

1 60 seconds in a minute   *sixty*
2 Mar 1 ....
3 Jul 5 ....
4 365 days in a year ....
5 1,440 minutes in a day ....
6 100 years in a century ....
7 Nov 22 ....

Was/Were

17 **Choose the correct options.**

A ¹ *Was /* (*Were*) you at school yesterday?
B Of course I ² *was / were*!
A What about Mary and John? ³ *Was / Were* they at school, too?
B I'm not sure. John ⁴ *was / were* at school all day, but Mary ⁵ *wasn't / weren't* in math class.
A What time ⁶ *was / were* that?
B Math class is from 11:30 to 12:30.
A ⁷ *Was / Were* all the other students in math?
B Three of the other girls ⁸ *wasn't / weren't* there. They had a special volleyball practice yesterday morning.

Opinion adjectives

18 **Complete the adjectives in these sentences.**

1 I hate this song. It's t*errible*.
2 That new horror movie is really s........................ !
3 This homework is so b........................ .
4 Yes, we scored! What an a........................ goal!
5 I'm sorry. That joke just isn't f........................ .
6 My mom loves r........................ books.
7 I think mountain biking is the most e........................ sport.
8 My little brother can be very a........................ .
9 This dress is too e........................ . I can't afford it.
10 This meal is really t........................ . Thanks!

Speaking and Listening

1 **Match the questions (1–5) to the answers (a–e).**
Then listen and check.

1 Do you have a favorite school subject? *d*
2 Do you live with your family?
3 Do you have any hobbies?
4 What kind of music do you like?
5 Were you at Tina's party last weekend?

a Yes, I was. We had a great time!
b Yes, I do. I live with my mother and my brother.
c I prefer dance music, and I also like soul.
d Yes. I really like art.
e Biking. I go out on my mountain bike every weekend.

2 **Complete the conversation with these phrases.**
Then listen and check.

~~Boring~~	so her classes	To the library
Very funny	What's happening	What subjects

Liam What class do you have next?
Sally Science!
Liam ¹ *Boring*!
Sally No, it isn't! I think science is really exciting.
Liam Not for me!
Sally ² .... do you like?
Liam Literature. And our geography teacher is fun, ³ .... are always interesting.
Sally True! Where are you going now?
Liam ⁴ .... , to do some research on the Internet.
Sally Oh, really? You mean watch videos?
Liam ⁵ .... ! You can't watch videos on the school computers.
Sally Anyway, are you going to Sonia's later?
Liam ⁶ .... at Sonia's?
Sally It's her birthday party!
Liam A party? Awesome! What time?
Sally Seven thirty. But you need to talk to Sonia first!

3 **Read the conversation in Exercise 2 again.**
Choose the correct options.

1 Sally (*likes*)*/ doesn't like* science.
2 Liam likes *two / three* different subjects.
3 Students *can / can't* watch videos in the library.
4 Sonia's party is *today / tomorrow*.

Home Sweet Home

Vocabulary • Rooms and parts of the house

★ **1** **Put these words in the correct column.**

| attic | balcony | driveway |
| landing | patio | yard |

inside the house		outside the house
attic		

★ **2** **Complete the sentences with the words from Exercise 1.**

1 Our car's in the garage! You can park in the *driveway*.
2 If you want to play ball, go and play in the .... !
3 All my old toys and books are up in the ....
4 We have a big plant on the .... at the top of the stairs.
5 In summer, we often have lunch out on the ....
6 There's an awesome view of the river from the .... outside my bedroom.

★★ **3** **Put the letters in the correct order to complete the text.**

It's a wonderful old house. The date above the door says 1820. We had to put on a new ¹ *roof* (foro) last year after the winter storms. The ² .... (ginslice) are high, and some of them are made of wood. There's a ³ .... (freeclapi) in each of the bedrooms, but we don't actually use them. When you go into the house, you go through the ⁴ .... (lalhywa), and the ⁵ .... (ratsis) are on the left. My mom's ⁶ .... (efocif) is behind them. It's the room with a lot of photos on the ⁷ .... (lawl). Oh, and the ⁸ .... (agrega) has space for two cars. That's on the left side of the building.

★★ **4** **Find the family treasure! Look at the picture. Complete the text with these words.**

| attic | fireplace | ~~hallway~~ | landing |
| office | roof | stairs | wall |

Go through the 1 *hallway* to the ² .... at the end. Then go up to the ³ .... on the second floor. Go left and find the room with a high ceiling. This is the ⁴ .... Inside, you can see a desk with a computer, a chair and some books in a bookcase. There's also a ⁵ .... in the middle, and in the ⁶ .... next to that, there's a small door. It's not easy to see this door because it looks just like a painting. Open the door and go up into the ⁷ .... Be careful because there's only one small window up there. At one end, there are a lot of old boxes. Under the ⁸ .... , on a shelf above the boxes, there's a large envelope. Take it down, open it and read what's inside!

Workbook page 116

Reading

★ (1) **Read the texts quickly. Choose the best option.**

The texts are …
a a leisure guide to the city.
b advertisements from people selling their homes.
c answers to people who want advice.

★ (2) **Complete the sentences.**

1 themansells says her husband has a new *job*.
2 jenwatts has no problems with .... her car.
3 benstarkey has a .... behind the house.
4 stellabailey lives near a baseball ....
5 jenwatts often travels by ....
6 benstarkey goes shopping by ....

★★ (3) **Complete the sentences with the correct name.**

1 *stellabailey* can see a nearby park from her home.
2 .... usually takes the train to Manhattan.
3 .... and .... live near some good stores.
4 .... doesn't use public transportation very much.
5 .... doesn't have any problems with noise.

Internet forum

themansells:

We're a family of four and we're looking for a new home in the city. My husband's going to work in a new office, and I'm a hairstylist. We have two young children. Any suggestions for a good area?

jenwatts:

We live in an apartment in Brooklyn, about twenty minutes from Manhattan. There are buses every fifteen minutes, so we don't need to use the car every day. Parking isn't a problem because the building has an underground garage. The shopping's good in this area.

benstarkey:

Our family lives in a house in Queens, about half an hour by train from Manhattan. It's a quiet area, without much traffic. We have a small front yard, and a backyard with a patio. The children are sitting out there right now! I only use the car to go shopping, and I park it in the driveway, so it's all very convenient.

stellabailey:

We live in a rented apartment in the Bronx, near Yankee Stadium. At the moment, people are coming out of a baseball game, so it's a little noisy, but it's not so bad at night. The stores and restaurants are good, and we can walk to most places. Oh, and there's a nice view of a nearby park from our balcony, too!

Grammar • Present simple and continuous

★ **(1)** **Read the text and choose the correct options.**

He ¹*(paints)* / *is painting* houses inside and outside. Today he ² *works* / *is working* in an apartment. First, he ³ *puts* / *is putting* all the furniture in the middle of the room. Then he ⁴ *covers* / *is covering* the furniture with a big cloth before he ⁵ *starts* / *is starting* work. At the moment, he ⁶ *paints* / *is painting* the edges around the ceiling.

★ **(2)** **Put the words in the correct order.**

1 Tom / Friday / goes / on / always / a / night / out
Tom always goes out on a Friday night.

2 housework / He / doesn't / with / help / the / usually
....
....

3 weekend / you / What / do / on / do / normally / the / ?
....
....

4 music / to / Elena's / MP3 / player / her / listening / on
....
....

5 reading / bus / on / isn't / a / magazine / She / the
....
....

6 now / are / What / doing / you / ?
....
....

★★ **(3)** **Look at the pictures and write sentences.**

1 work / café / serve / coffee
He works in a café, and now he's serving coffee.

2 live / small town / visit / city
....

3 sell / fish / talk / phone
....

4 repair / cars / take / break
....

5 drive / taxi / take passenger / station
....

★★ **(4)** **Complete the conversation with the Present simple or Present continuous form of the verbs.**

A Mike, is that you? Are you busy?

M Yes! (I/make) ¹ *I'm making* dinner in the kitchen.

A You in the kitchen? But (you/not normally/cook) ² ....
.... ! Why (you/cook) ³ .... today?

M Because my (girlfriend/come over) ⁴ ....
for dinner.

A So is it Italian food?

M No, it isn't. (We/only/have) ⁵ ....
Italian food in restaurants. This is a special Indian meal.

A (you/mean) ⁶ .... Indian from India?

M Yes, of course!

A But isn't that very spicy food?

M Often, yes, but (it/not always/have to) ⁷ ....
.... be hot!

A OK! Anyway, what's that funny noise I can hear?

M Oh no! The (meat/burn) ⁸ ....
in the pot! That's what happens when I talk too much on the phone!

★ 5 **Make questions for the underlined answers.**

1 The children are playing in <u>the attic</u>.
Where are the children playing?

2 Right now, we're <u>having a party in the garage</u>!
....
....

3 My sister's <u>studying abroad</u> this year.
....
....

4 Tom's talking to <u>a friend</u> right now.
....
....

5 I'm waiting for <u>a bus</u>.
....
....

6 My dad mows the lawn <u>every two weeks</u>.
....
....

7 We <u>clean the house</u> in the spring.
....
....

8 Yes, we do. <u>We have a fireplace</u> in the living room.
....
....

9 Kevin usually celebrates his birthday <u>in the basement</u>!
....
....

Vocabulary • Furniture and household objects

★ 1 **Label the numbered objects in the picture.**

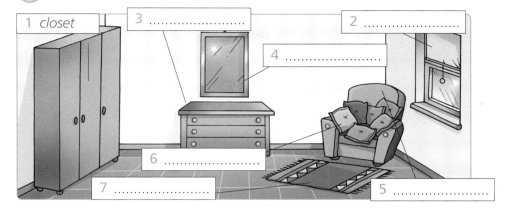

1 *closet*
3 ....
2 ....
4 ....
6 ....
7 ....
5 ....

★ 2 **Complete the sentences with the words from Exercise 1.**

1 The *rug* is on the floor.
2 In front of the left wall, you can see a ....
3 In the corner of the room, there's an .... with .... on it.
4 Near the armchair, you can see a window with a ....
5 On the back wall, there's a .... with a .... above it.

★ 3 **Match these words to the definitions (1–6).**

| alarm clock   bookcase   ~~curtains~~   comforter   pillow   vase |

1 We normally use two of these to cover a window.   *curtains*
2 We use this to wake up on time in the morning.   ....
3 We use this to keep warm in bed.   ....
4 We usually put flowers in one of these.   ....
5 We use this in bed for our head.   ....
6 We keep books and magazines in this.   ....

★★ 4 **Put the letters in the correct order to complete the text.**

This apartment's not bad! It has a big [1] *closet* (tesloc) for my clothes, and there's a [2] .... (koboseca) in the living room. I need that for my books because this month I'm taking a computer science course. And there's a desk but no [3] .... (cramhira), but I can bring one from home. What else? There's a [4] .... (rorimr) in the bathroom, but I don't see any [5] .... (stranuci) on the window, so maybe I can ask my mom to buy some. I don't like all those [6] .... (nisshuco) on the sofa—they can go in the closet in the bedroom. The bed's OK, but I'll bring my own [7] .... (remoctorf) and a couple of [8] .... (lowlips) because I'm more comfortable that way.

Grammar Reference pages 108–109   **Workbook** page 116

Chatroom Describing a place

Speaking and Listening

★ **1** Match the questions (1–6) to the answers (a–f). Then listen and check.

1 What's your school like?   *d*
2 What's your bedroom like?
3 What's that new shopping mall like?
4 What's your vacation home like?
5 What's Paula's hometown like?
6 What's that new café on Osmond Street like?

a It's very modern. It has three floors and a café on the roof.
b It's a little small, but they have really good music.
c It's pretty old, it's on the tenth floor, and it has great views.
d It's really big, with more than a thousand students.
e It's very big and really busy, with a lot of stores and traffic.
f It's pretty small, but very comfortable, and I have all my photos on the wall.

★ **2** Put the conversation in the correct order.

a And what's your room like?   ....
b So where are you living now?   *1*
c Are you happy with it then?   ....
d It's very noisy and a little strange.   ....
e What's the city like?   ....
f Yes, but it's a long way from downtown!   ....
g In a rented room in the city.   ....
h Well, it's really cheap and pretty big.   ....

★★ **3** Complete the conversation with these phrases. Then listen and check.

| a little small | ~~Do you mean~~ | it like | kind of strange |
| pretty far | really wonderful | the house like | very big |

Olga   Hey, Tammi! How are you? I haven't seen you for a while!
Tammi   Hi, Olga! I'm just visiting and doing some shopping.
Olga   ¹ *Do you mean* you don't live here anymore?
Tammi   Well, we have a new house on the coast, but I still come to visit my grandparents.
Olga   That's very good news! What's ² .... ?
Tammi   It's not ³ ...., just two floors, but it's in a really nice area.
Olga   I'm sure! And does it have ocean views?
Tammi   Yes. You can see ⁴ .... from the balcony upstairs. And it has a swimming pool too, but it's ⁵ ....
Olga   And what about the town? What's ⁶ .... ?
Tammi   Well, the house is ⁷ .... because it's five minutes from the beach. But the town is ⁸ ...., and my brothers and I miss our friends.

★ **4** Listen to the conversation in Exercise 3 again. Choose the correct options.

1 Olga and Tammi (know) / don't know each other.
2 Tammi *lives* / *doesn't live* with her grandparents.
3 Tammi likes the *location* / *size* of the house.
4 The balcony has *good* / *bad* views.
5 The house is *far from* / *near* the beach.
6 The children are *very happy* / *a little uncomfortable* in the new town.

★★ **5** Answer the questions about yourself.

1 What's your city or town like?   ....
2 What's your school like?   ....
3 What's your street like?   ....
4 What's your home like?   ....
5 What's your room like?   ....

Speaking and Listening page 120

Grammar • Verb + -ing

★ 1 **Complete the text with the correct form of these verbs.**

be	get	go	listen
rent	~~see~~	watch	

Living here is very easy. We enjoy ¹*seeing* the sunshine almost every day, and we love ² .... able to sit outside for meals. We also like ³ .... for long walks in the countryside, which is close to our apartment. And we don't mind ⁴ .... wet when it rains, because it doesn't rain very often. As for going out at night, there are several movie theaters, although we sometimes prefer ⁵ .... a DVD at home. There's a theater too, although we don't go very often. I can't stand ⁶ .... musicals and I don't like ⁷ .... to classical music either!

★ 2 **Put the words in the correct order.**

1 apartment / I / stand / ground / living / in / an / on / the / can't / floor
I can't stand living in an apartment on the ground floor.

2 with / sleeping / on / She / the / light / prefers
....
....

3 watching / all / Grandma / TV / day / enjoys
....
....

4 housework / with / brother / hates / helping / the / My
....

★★ 3 **Write sentences.**

A Do you like living in Athens?
B I / enjoy / live / a big city
¹ *I enjoy living in a big city.*
A And what about the weather?
B I / love / sit / outside in the sun!
² ....
A And the traffic?
B I / not stand / drive / with so many cars / in the streets!
³ ....
A So how do you get around the city?
B I / like / ride / my bicycle!
⁴ ....
A What about the food?
B I / not mind / try / new foods!
⁵ ....
A And the language?
B I / prefer / speak / English!
⁶ ....
Greek is very difficult for me!

★★ 4 **Write sentences. Use the information in the table.**

	😊😊 loves	😊 likes/enjoys	😐 doesn't mind	😞😞 hates/ can't stand
Justin	1 play video games	2 take the dog for a walk	3 wash the car	4 do housework
Leonor	5 get up late on the weekend	6 text on her cell phone	7 help her sister with her homework	8 clean the bathrooom

1 *Justin loves playing video games.*
2 ....
3 ....
4 ....
5 ....
6 ....
7 ....
8 ....

Grammar Reference pages 108–109

Reading

1 **Read the texts quickly. Match the text types (1–3) to the texts (A–C).**

1 a postcard
2 a tourist advertisement
3 an offer of accommodation

Fuengirola A

in the heart of the Costa del Sol

Welcome to Fuengirola in the heart of the Costa del Sol, an ideal vacation destination! In winter, it's a quiet town of 72,000 inhabitants, with very fresh seafood and interesting places to visit. It's ideal for older people. In summer, it's a fantastic place for sun, sand and sea, with a population of 250,000 people! It's very popular with families and young people because there is so much to see and do. With shopping, restaurants, clubs, parks and a zoo—it has nearly everything!

B

VACATION APARTMENT FOR RENT in Fuengirola, southern Spain. Large apartment available for July and August. Three bedrooms, two bathrooms, kitchen and living room. Complete with balcony, underground garage and elevator. Fully furnished with beds, a sofa, armchairs and a TV. The kitchen's a little small, but most visitors eat out. For more information, please email fun_fuengirola@costadelsol.com.

C

Dear Mom and Dad,

Here we are, finally at the beach! The house we're sharing with friends is small, but we only come back here to shower and change before going out again. Maggie says she hates sitting on the beach all day, so she's doing a lot of sports. Tom loves doing nothing, so he enjoys lying on the beach and then going out at night. And I prefer doing a little of everything, so I read, listen to music, go swimming, go shopping ... and just relax! The weather's a little hot for me, so I don't go to the beach in the afternoon, but I'm having a wonderful time!

Love,
Linda

2 **Complete the sentences.**

1 Fuengirola has a lot of *older* visitors in winter.
2 In summer, 250,000 people .... in Fuengirola.
3 .... people can sleep in the apartment.
4 The apartment has an .... garage.
5 Linda and her friends don't .... much time in the house.
6 Linda .... go to the beach in the afternoon.

Listening

1 6 **Listen to the conversation and decide who is talking.**

1 a brother and sister
2 two friends
3 two office workers

2 6 **Listen again. Choose the correct options.**

1 The boy prefers the room *with* / *without* the balcony.
2 The girl *likes* / *doesn't like* the room with the closet.
3 The second room has a *bookcase* / *desk*.
4 The girl would like to have the *dresser* / *mirror*.
5 The boy wants a *dresser* / *desk*.

Writing • A description of a room

1 **Rewrite the sentences. Use the linking words.**

1 I like playing in the attic. I like playing in the basement.   (and)
I like playing in the attic and the basement.

2 We enjoy sitting on the balcony. We like sitting on the patio.   (also)

....
....

3 The cat loves hiding behind the armchairs. He's afraid of going down to the basement.   (but)

....
....

4 That's his favorite pillow. He doesn't like using a comforter.   (however)

....
....

5 We like having pillow fights. We like playing with cushions.   (too)

....
....

6 I love lying on the floor to read. Sheena loves looking at the photos on the walls.   (and)

....
....

2 **Look at the picture. Read the text. Correct four mistakes in the text.**

My dream room looks like this. It's pretty big and bright, and I can organize it the way I want.

The best things in the room are the bed with its comforter and the rug next to it. Opposite the bed is a bookcase with a TV on one of the shelves. On the wall above the bed there are posters of my favorite musicians and artists. There's a desk in the corner under a window. When I need to study, I just close the blind. On the wall, to the left of the window, there's a board for photos and notes. My papers and school stuff go in the drawers on the right of the desk.

I can lie on the bed listening to music. However, I also need time at my desk. When friends visit, we can play games on the TV, too.

3 **Read the room description again. Put these details in the correct section in column A.**

bright	lie on the bed
papers in the drawers	play video games
~~posters on the wall~~	pretty big

	A Picture room	**B My dream room**
Introduction		*My dream room has …*
Furniture and walls	*posters on the wall*	*There is/are …*
Activities		*I can …*

4 **Think of your dream room. Write phrases about it in column B.**

5 **Write a description of your dream room. Use your ideas and information from Exercises 3 and 4.**

2 What's the Story?

Vocabulary • Adjectives to describe pictures

★ **1** Put these words in the correct column.

beautiful	blurry	boring	colorful	dark	dramatic
fake	funny	horrible	interesting	old-fashioned	silly

one syllable	two syllables	three syllables
dark	blurry	beautiful

★ **2** Match the words (1–5) to the definitions (a–e).

1 blurry *e*
2 boring
3 fake
4 dramatic
5 old-fashioned

a From another period in time, when life was very different
b It's uninteresting.
c It's not real.
d It's exciting; it makes me want to look at it.
e It's not clear; I can't see it very well.

★★ **3** Complete the conversation with these words.

blurry	boring	dramatic	fake	old-fashioned	silly

A Look at this! Look at those clothes! And the hairstyles!
B Where did you find that?
A In a box in the attic. The pictures are really [1] *old-fashioned*.
B Yeah. I think they must be from the war or something.
A They're pretty [2] .... ! There aren't any colors.
B Yes, but sometimes they're very [3] .... Here's one of a building on fire.
A And what's this one?
B I don't know! It's [4] .... , so I can't see the detail. It looks like a photo of a person's foot.
A Well, that's a [5] .... photo! Why would anyone do that?!
B Who knows! What about this one? It says "Love from Mount Everest, 1945."
A That's a [6] .... photo! Nobody climbed Mount Everest until 1953!

★★ **4** Put the letters in the correct order to complete the text.

There are many computer programs for working with photos. Users can create many kinds of [1] *interesting* (gritsentien) pictures and effects with the software. You can completely change a [2] .... (floroluc) image by replacing the normal colors with a kind of brown, so you make the image look [3] .... (lod-fadishneo). Or you can change the clothes a person is wearing, and make the picture [4] .... (nunfy). Or again, you can make parts of the image [5] .... (ylrurb), so that one part becomes more [6] .... (cardamit). As people say, the only limit is your imagination! The only problem, however, is that it becomes difficult to tell the difference between an original and a [7] .... (kefa) photo!

Workbook page 117

Reading

★ 1 Match the photos (A–C) to the paragraphs (1–3).

★ 2 Complete the sentences.

1 Ulrike *changed* her clothes.
2 In the photo, Danny was ....
3 A storm .... into the beach last weekend.
4 Danny had his party in a ....
5 A tree .... on some cars.
6 Ulrike wasn't .... to the other people in the group.

★ 3 Are the statements true (T) or false (F)?

1 There were a lot of people at Danny's party.   *T*
2 Danny's neighbors weren't happy about the music.   ....
3 Ulrike's group went to the beach last weekend.   ....
4 Nothing in Ulrike's backpack was dry.   ....
5 People at the beach were prepared for the storm.   ....
6 No one was hurt in the accident.   ....

Brain Trainer

Underline all the adjectives in comments 1, 2 and 3.

What do you notice about
a) their form?
b) their position?

Photos	Comments

A

1 Hi, guys! Here's a nice (but blurry) picture of Danny's birthday party! He was dancing really fast! There were about forty of us there. We used his parents' garage for the party. We stayed late, but nobody complained about the music. It was great!

B

2 Hey, everyone! Here are some colorful pictures from our hiking trip last weekend. My favorite one is of Ulrike falling into the water. She was crossing the stream and listening to music on her MP3 player. She didn't hear us warn her about the moving stones, so she fell in. She didn't hurt herself, but her backpack got wet, and everything inside it did, too. She changed into some dry clothes that Maria gave her.

C

3 How about this for a dramatic picture? We were at the beach last weekend when a sudden storm came in. The winds were really strong, so we left the beach fast. Then a big palm tree fell on some cars parked in the street. Luckily, there was no one in the cars. Adrian took this picture just five minutes after it happened.

Grammar • Past simple

★ **1** Match the questions (1–4) to the answers (a–d).

1 Who took these photos?   *b*
2 Where did she take them?
3 What happened in this one?
4 Did they come out all right?

a Most of them did, but some are a little blurry.
b Jane did.
c It was at Fran's house, on Saturday.
d The flash didn't work!

★★ **2** Complete the text with the correct form of the verbs.

This is a photo of my grandmother, who had an interesting life. When she was fourteen, the war started, and the family ¹ *lost* (lose) their business in the city. Her parents ² .... (not want) to stay in Wales, so they ³ .... (sail) to Argentina. They ⁴ .... (not speak) Spanish, but there was a Welsh community in Argentina, and her father ⁵ .... (find) a job there. My grandmother ⁶ .... (study) in Buenos Aires, where she ⁷ .... (meet) my grandfather. They got married three years later and had three children, including my father.

★★ **3** Make sentences about Tanya's week. Use the information in the table.

Things to do	Done ✓	Not done ✗
1 clean my room	✓	
2 wash Dad's car		✗
3 make birthday cake		✗
4 buy new shirt	✓	
5 reply to emails	✓	
6 check exam grades		✗
7 clean the fireplace	✓	

1 *She cleaned her room.*
2 ....
3 ....
4 ....
5 ....
6 ....
7 ....

• Past continuous

★ **4** Put the words in the correct order to make answers.

1 A Where were you last weekend?
   B on / I / the / volleyball / playing / was / beach
   I was playing volleyball on the beach.
2 A What about Saturday night?
   B club / I / friends / dancing / some / at / was / the / with
   ....
3 A Very interesting! And on Sunday morning?
   B newspapers / We / the /were / morning / reading / all
   ....
4 A And on Sunday afternoon, were you walking in the park?
   B We / park / walking / in / the / on / weren't / Sunday
   ....
5 A So what were you doing on Sunday?
   B We / an / old-fashioned / watching / were / on / movie / TV
   ....
6 A What were the people in the movie doing?
   B acting / silly / were / They
   ....

★★ **5** Make sentences with the Past continuous form of the verbs.

1 Some children / play / in the yard
   Some children were playing in the yard.
2 A dog / run / in the park
   ....
3 A man / park / his car
   ....
4 A young couple / do / their shopping
   ....
5 Some friends / take / photos
   ....
6 A neighbor / wash / his car
   ....
7 A cat / drink / milk
   ....

Grammar Reference pages 110–111

Vocabulary • Adjective + preposition

★ 1 Match the sentence beginnings (1–6) to the endings (a–f).

1 Stella's really good   *e*
2 Brian's very interested
3 Old-fashioned pictures are popular
4 Ella's excited
5 We're very proud
6 Jane's bored

a with some collectors.
b with the music on her MP3 player.
c in animal photography.
d of our school's prize in the photo competition.
e at taking dramatic photos.
f about seeing her photos in the school magazine.

★ 2 Choose the correct options.

1 We don't want to go to the mall because we're *proud of / tired of* going there!
2 Don't turn the light off! I'm *afraid of / bad at* the dark.
3 Our team won the game and we were *excited about / angry with* it.
4 She's a very nice person and she's *popular with / proud of* the other students.
5 Our teacher is really *good at / sorry for* telling stories.
6 I want to study music because I am really *bad at / interested in* it.

★★ 3 Complete the sentences with these words.

| ~~afraid~~ angry excited interested bad sorry |

1 Everyone said they were *afraid* of traffic accidents.
2 He was .... with them because he didn't get a prize.
3 I'm usually .... at science, but I did very well on my last exam.
4 Everyone is .... about the next Olympic Games.
5 She was .... in becoming a writer.
6 Everyone felt .... for the parents with the sick children.

★★ 4 Complete the text with the correct prepositions.

This is an interesting picture! You can see this boy on the left: he looks tired ¹ *of* playing with his toys. And the girl on the right, who looks bored ² .... her doll's house. The other children in the middle are laughing and pointing at the screen. It looks like they're very excited ³ .... a video game. And look at the grandmother's face. She's very proud ⁴ .... her grandchildren! Finally, I feel sorry ⁵ .... the dog next to the boy. It looks afraid ⁶ .... the image of itself in the mirror! This is a nice picture because it is full of interesting details.

Workbook page 117

Chatroom Permission

Speaking and Listening

★ **1** Put the words in order to make questions. Then listen and check.
7

1 Lena / us / you / comes / mind / if / Do / with / ?
Do you mind if Lena comes with us?

2 bicycle / borrow / Can / your / I / ?

....

....

3 if / it / dog / we / OK / take / Is / the / ?

....

....

★ **2** Complete the conversation with the questions from Exercise 1. Then listen and check.
8

A Uncle John! ª.........................

....

B What do you want it for?

A Kurt and I want to go for a ride.

B Yes, you can. Just be careful with the traffic.

A ᵇ...

....

B Yes, of course! He needs the exercise.

A ᶜ*Do you mind if Lena comes with us?*

B Yes, I do! She has an exam in the morning, and she has to study!

★★ **3** Complete the conversation with these words. Then listen and check.
9

Do you mind if	I'm sorry	Is it OK	of course
~~popular with~~	you can		

Guide	Good morning and welcome to the Milefoot Country Park! This park is very ¹*popular with* people who love the countryside. We hope you enjoy your visit.
Man	Can we take photos in the park?
Guide	Yes, ².......................... . But we recommend that you don't go too near the animals.
Woman	Is it OK if we have a picnic somewhere?
Guide	Yes, ³.......................... . There are special areas with benches where visitors can eat and drink.
Boy	⁴.......................... if we go fishing in the river?
Guide	No, I'm sorry, it isn't. The fish are protected, and you can't catch them.
Boy	What about a barbecue? ⁵.......................... we have a barbecue?
Guide	We don't mind if you have picnics, but ⁶.........................., you can't have barbecues. It's too dangerous to light fires in the park.

★★ **4** Listen to the conversation in Exercise 3 again. Choose the correct options.
9

1 You (can) / can't see animals in the park.
2 Visitors *should* / *shouldn't* go near the animals.
3 Visitors can have picnics *anywhere in the park* / *in special areas*.
4 Fishing *is* / *isn't* possible.
5 Fires *are* / *aren't* allowed in the park.

★★ **5** Write a conversation. Use phrases from Exercises 1–3 above and this information:

You are staying for the weekend at a friend's house.
Ask permission to do three different things. Remember to include your friend's replies.

Speaking and Listening page 121

Grammar • Past simple vs Past continuous

★ **1** **Match the sentence beginnings (1–5) to the endings (a–e).**

1 I was having a wonderful dream   *d*
2 A ball hit a woman
3 The girl was texting on her phone
4 The boys saw a bank robbery
5 We were watching a news report on TV

a while they were sitting on the balcony.
b while she was walking through the park.
c when we recognized our friends at a concert.
d when the alarm clock woke me up.
e when she put her foot in a hole.

★ **2** **Choose the correct options.**

1 The weather *changed* / *was changing* while we *came* / *were coming* down the mountain.
2 We *ran* / *were running* through the woods when Angelica *fell* / *was falling*.
3 A bird *landed* / *was landing* on my shoulder while I *ate* / *was eating* a sandwich!
4 Marla *watched* / *was watching* TV when her friend *arrived* / *was arriving*.
5 I *got* / *was getting* a call while I *waited* / *was waiting* for the bus.
6 The passengers *sang* / *were singing* when the plane *took off* / *was taking off*.

★★ **3** **Make questions for the underlined answers.**

1 I was <u>listening to the radio</u> when I heard the news.
What were you doing when you heard the news?
2 I was listening to the radio when <u>I heard the news</u>.
What happened while you were listening to the radio?
3 Thieves were stealing a painting when <u>the police arrived</u>.
....
4 Thieves were <u>stealing a painting</u> when the police arrived.
....
5 My parents were <u>driving home</u> when the storm started.
....
6 My parents were driving home when <u>the storm started</u>.
....
7 Tania was <u>living abroad</u> when her parents moved.
....
8 Tania was living abroad when <u>her parents moved</u>.
....
9 I was <u>recording the concert</u> when the battery died.
....
10 I was recording the concert when <u>the battery died</u>.
....

★★ **4** **Make questions for the missing information.**

1 I was .... when I heard the news.
What were you doing when you heard the news?
2 Our team was .... when the rain started.
....
3 We were .... when the battery died.
....
4 Ana was .... when the phone rang.
....
5 My parents were .... when the mail carrier arrived.
....
6 The students were .... when the teacher entered the room.
....

Brain Trainer

Put *when* or *while* into these sentences:

I was drinking my coffee .... the email arrived.
The email arrived .... I was drinking my coffee.
Can you use either word in both sentences?
Look at Grammar Reference page 110 and write the rule.

Grammar Reference pages 110–111

Reading

1 Read the text quickly. Choose the best title.

a A Fun Trip to the UK
b A Dramatic Trip to the UK
c A Boring Trip to the UK

In the spring of 2010, my family was preparing for a trip to the UK. We wanted to go to Scotland to visit Edinburgh, and then to stay in London, to see all the famous places there. We were planning to stay for ten days, and I was really looking forward to the trip.
On April 10, we flew to Edinburgh and took a taxi to the hotel. The weather was colder than at home, but it was clear and bright. The next three days we went sightseeing. The dungeons on the Royal Mile were really cool! The 14th was our last day there, so we went shopping on the famous Princes Street. I got a photo of myself with a bagpiper in his kilt, and I emailed it to my friends. In the evening, we were having dinner when we saw pictures on TV of a volcano erupting in Iceland. The pictures were pretty dramatic, but we didn't worry.
The next day, we arrived at the airport for the flight to London. But we didn't catch the plane because all the flights were canceled. Why? Because the ash from the volcano was a serious problem for planes flying over the UK! In the end, we had to take a train to London, and we spent a whole week sightseeing and shopping in all the famous places. But we had to wait another two days before we could finally catch a flight home. Of course, that was OK with me, since I had an extra two days of vacation!

2 Read the text again. Put these events in the correct order.

a go back to Edinburgh
airport   ....
b visit London   ....
c arrive in Edinburgh   .1..
d see a volcanic eruption
on TV   ....
e visit the dungeons   ....
f go shopping on
Princes Street   ....

Listening

1 Listen to an interview with a girl who wants to be a photographer. How many photos do they talk about?
10

a 2   b 3   c 4

2 Listen again and choose the correct options.
10

1 The photo was of her
brother's .... birthday.
a second
b third
c fourth
2 The bird caught a .... .
a mouse
b rabbit
c cat
3 She took the photo in
Vermont in the .... .
a spring
b fall
c winter
4 The colors in the photo
were .... .
a on the buildings
b on an umbrella
c in the streets
5 The two women in the photo
were .... .
a friends
b sisters
c mother and daughter

Writing • A description of a picture

1 **Read the text and correct the sentences.**

My mom took this photo about two years ago, when we were visiting my uncle. He lives in Spain, so we don't often see each other. He was living in a new house, and it was the first time that we saw it.

The photo is of a special meal. We cooked paella, which his family had never tried before. The weather was great, so we ate outside. You can see grass and some trees in the background. That's the food on the table in the foreground. That's my uncle and my cousin on the right, and my aunt on the left serving the food. My sister and I are in the middle. We're all laughing because my uncle was telling a joke.
I like this photo because it brings back good memories of the time we spent together.

1 This was the family's third visit to the uncle's house.
This was the family's first visit to the uncle's house.

2 They ate in the kitchen.
....

3 The food is on the table in the background.
....

4 The people in the photo are crying.
....

5 Her uncle is on the left of the photo.
....

2 **Read the text again. Put these phrases in the correct place in column A.**

a special meal	good memories
in the background	in the foreground
in the middle	meal outside
new house	on the left
on the right	time together
~~two years ago~~	visit my uncle

	A Picture description	B My photo
Introduction	*two years ago*	
Who's/What's in the photo and where		
Reasons for choosing the photo		

3 **Choose your favorite photo. Write phrases about it in column B.**

4 **Write a description of your photo. Use your ideas and information from Exercises 2 and 3.**

(Introduction)
....
....
....

(Description)
....
....
....
....
....

(Conclusion)
....
....
....

3 It's a Bargain!

Vocabulary • Shopping nouns

★ 1 Match (1–6) to (a–f) to make nouns.

1 dollar   a vendor
2 down   b basket
3 fruit   c bill
4 market   d stand
5 sales   e town
6 shopping   f person

★ 2 Complete the sentences with the nouns from Exercise 1.

1 We often go to the market. One of our friends is a *market vendor* there!
2 When you enter our supermarket, please take a ....
3 The best stores here are ....
4 Do you need money? The nearest .... is opposite the bus station.
5 Let's meet at the .... where they sell peaches.
6 We asked the .... where to find the sports department.

★ 3 Match these words to the definitions (1–6).

bargain	change	customer
line	products	~~sale~~

1 This is a special time when store prices are cheaper.   *sale*
2 This is the name for the things we buy in stores.   ....
3 This is the money you get back if you pay too much.   ....
4 This is when you buy something good at a very low price.   ....
5 This is the name for the person who wants to buy something.   ....
6 This is where you have to wait when there are a lot of people who want to do the same thing.   ....

Workbook page 118

★★ 4 Complete the text with these words.

~~ATM~~	bills	change	coin
line	market stand	price	vendor

At about 11 o'clock, he stopped at an ¹ATM to get some money. He had to wait in ² .... for a while. Then he put the ³ .... in his wallet. Next, he went to a ⁴ .... where they were selling shoes. But he didn't buy any. The ⁵ .... didn't look very happy. Maybe there was a problem with the ⁶ .... A small boy near the stand was asking for money. I saw the man give the boy a ⁷ .... Then he went to a café, where he talked on his cell phone. When he finished his coffee, he paid the waiter and left the ⁸ .... on the table.

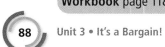

Reading

Markets or Supermarkets?

At *Shopping Trends* magazine, we asked for our readers' opinions, and here is what they said.

Well, I live in a quiet, small town without many stores, and no market. The nearest market is in the city half an hour away, and there aren't enough buses to get there. So for me, supermarkets are the best option. I can simply park the car and do the shopping. It's more convenient, and there's a greater variety of products than at a market. And markets, for me personally, aren't clean enough.

Sandra

There's a good market near my apartment, so it's easier for me to do my shopping there. Prices are about the same as at the supermarket, but the service is better. I only go to the supermarket when the market is closed.

Trish

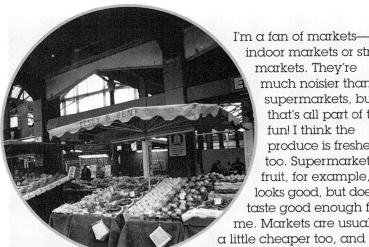

I'm a fan of markets—indoor markets or street markets. They're much noisier than supermarkets, but that's all part of the fun! I think the produce is fresher, too. Supermarket fruit, for example, looks good, but doesn't taste good enough for me. Markets are usually a little cheaper too, and always friendlier. The vendors know me, so they know what I want.

Matt

★ **(1)** **Write the correct names.**

1 .... clearly prefers markets.
2 .... clearly prefers supermarkets.
3 .... prefers markets, but shops at both.

★ **(2)** **Complete the sentences.**

1 There isn't a *market* where Sandra lives.
2 Trish likes the .... she gets at the market.
3 Matt prefers the .... food they sell in markets.
4 Trish goes to the supermarket when the market is ....
5 Matt likes markets because they are .... and friendlier.

★★ **(3)** **Choose the correct option.**

1 (Sandra) / Matt thinks markets are a little dirty.
2 Trish / Matt prefers the fruit from markets.
3 Sandra / Trish thinks that prices are very similar.
4 Trish / Matt knows that supermarkets are quieter places to shop in.
5 Sandra / Matt doesn't have a market near her/his home.
6 Sandra / Trish can't always get to the market when it's open.

Grammar • Comparatives and superlatives

★ 1 **Put the words in the correct order.**

1 sister's / is / mine / comfortable / My / than / room / more
My sister's room is more comfortable than mine.

2 town / are / the / beach / The / nearer / our / mountains / than / to

....

....

3 store / in / is / the / town / Benson's / cheapest

....

....

4 market stand / best / has / This / the / products

....

....

5 world / popular / the / The / most / Internet / market / the / is / in

....

....

6 bargains / supermarket / The / has / than / our / stores / better / local

....

....

★★ 2 **Complete the text with the correct form of the adjectives.**

My parents say it's important to save money when we buy things. Clothes and shoes are often ¹*cheaper* (cheap) in the street market, but regular stores usually have ².......................
(good) quality. The local department store always has the ³....................... (good) selection, but it's also the ⁴....................... (expensive) store in town! However, they have the ⁵....................... (popular) sales too, because you can find really good bargains there. My friends say it's ⁶....................... (easy) to do all the shopping in one big store, but I say it's ⁷....................... (interesting) to visit different places and compare prices and quality.

★★ 3 **Write sentences. Use the information in the table.**

	Todds	Ekomart	Breezer
Distance from downtown	0.5 km	1.5 km	4 km
Service (good)	✶✶	✶✶✶	✶
Salespeople (friendly)	✶	✶✶	✶✶✶
Prices (expensive)	✶✶✶	✶✶	✶

(✶ = minimum)

1 Ekomart / Todds / distance
Ekomart is farther from downtown than Todds.

2 Ekomart / Todds / service

....

3 Breezer / Todds / service

....

4 Ekomart / Todds / salespeople

....

5 Ekomart / Breezer / prices

....

6 Breezer / distance
Breezer is the farthest from downtown.

7 Todds / prices

....

• *Too and enough*

★ 4 **Complete the conversation with *too* or *enough*.**

A Do you want to go swimming?

B Not really! It's ¹*too* cold today. How about going to the movies?

A I can't. I don't have ²..................... money.

B Then let's go biking!

A I'm ³....................... tired! I played soccer all afternoon yesterday. What did you do?

B My homework. I didn't have ⁴.....................
time to do anything else.

A OK! Was that your math homework?

B Yes, it was.

A Great! So you can help me with mine. I tried, but it was ⁵....................... difficult.

B I'm not sure about that. Your problem is that you don't have ⁶....................... patience!

★ (5) **Kelly doesn't want to go to Dylan's party. Write sentences using *too* or *enough*.**

Sorry, Dylan, but …

1 party / end / late.
the party ends too late.

2 I / busy / at home

....
....

3 I / not have / time

....
....

4 your apartment / far / my house

....
....

5 bus / not stop / near

....
....

6 I / not have / money / buy / a present

....
....

7 party dress / not new

....
....

8 I / tired

....
....

Vocabulary • Money verbs

★ (1) **Match the sentence beginnings (1–5) to the endings (a–e).**

1 Good morning! I'd like to borrow
2 How would you like to pay
3 Excuse me! Do these cost
4 Teri's family is going to sell
5 I always pay for gas

a $6.50 or $8.50?
b by credit card.
c their house.
d for your new suit?
e some money for a Porsche.

★ (2) **Complete the advertisements with these verbs.**

afford   lend   pay in cash   ~~Buy~~   Save   Win

1 Buy **2, get 1 free!**

2 .... HUNDREDS of prizes in our new competition!

3 .... *$50 with our special offers!*

4 **Best prices in town for your old cell phones! We .... !**

5 **Do you need money urgently? We .... instant cash! ASK INSIDE.**

6 WINTER SALES … AT PRICES YOU CAN .... !

★★ (3) **Choose the correct options.**

1 Did you know? Your brother *won* / *earned* a new bicycle in a competition!
2 Tamara needed money for the trip, so I *borrowed* / *lent* her $50.
3 She *bought* / *cost* her mother a new watch for her birthday.
4 Ellen *paid* / *sold* her old laptop for $40.
5 It wasn't very expensive, so we *afforded* / *paid in cash*.
6 The new store was fantastic! I *earned* / *spent* $80 on T-shirts for my friends.

★★ (4) **Complete the text with these verbs.**

afford   borrowed   ~~cost~~   earned   paid by credit card   saved

Paula wanted a new smart phone, but it ¹*cost* $500, and she couldn't ²..................... it. She ³..................... the money from her birthday presents, she ⁴..................... some extra money by doing some work for the neighbors, and she ⁵..................... the last $50 from her mother. Finally, she and her mother went to the store, and her mother ⁶..................... . Paula's mother says it's better to do that because sometimes there are problems with the products you buy.

Grammar Reference pages 112–113

Workbook page 118

Speaking and Listening

★ **(1)** **Match the questions (1–6) to the answers (a–f). Then listen and check.**
11

1 Could you give me change for the coffee machine ? *c*
2 Would you mind taking a photo for us?
3 Can you pass me the sugar?
4 Could you give me a hand with these boxes?
5 Would you mind driving me to the station?
6 Could you mail this letter for me?

a Sorry, I can't. I don't drive.
b Sure. Do you want a spoon, too?
c Sorry, I can't. I only have bills.
d OK. There's a post office next to my school.
e No problem. Where are you going to stand?
f Sorry, I can't. I have a pain in my back.

★ **(2)** **Put the conversation in the correct order. Then listen and check.**
12

a Good idea! Can you get them? They're too high for me. ....
b I think so. Would you mind paying for this? ....
c What about some of those snacks? ....
d Sorry, I can't. I don't have any cash. ....
e What else do we need for the party? *1*
f Sure. Is that everything? ....

★ **(3)** **Complete the conversation with these words. Then listen and check.**
13

| ~~Can~~ | Could | give | mind | problem | Sorry |

Lucy	Olivia!
Olivia	What?
Lucy	¹ *Can* you help me choose a camera? I don't know which one to buy.
Olivia	OK. What kind do you prefer?
Lucy	I want one I can use in the swimming pool.
Olivia	I don't know about those! Let's ask the salesperson. Excuse me! ² .... you show us some cameras for taking pictures underwater?
Salesperson	No ³ .... ! This one is very popular.
Lucy	Would you ⁴ .... taking a photo for us?
Salesperson	⁵ .... , I can't. You have to buy the camera first!
Lucy	What do you think, Olivia?
Olivia	It's your money!
Lucy	OK, I'll buy it. Can you ⁶ .... me a hand with these bags? I need to find my money.
Olivia	Sure!

★★ **(4)** **Listen to the conversation in Exercise 3 again. Complete the sentences with one word.**
13

1 Lucy wants to *buy* a new camera.
2 She asks Olivia to .... her choose one.
3 They decide to ask the ....
4 They also ask her to .... a photo for them.
5 But the salesperson says that's not ....
6 In the end, Lucy .... to buy the camera.

★★ **(5)** **Write a conversation. Use phrases from Exercises 1–3 and this information:**

You are shopping for clothes with a friend. Ask your friend to help you decide on three different items. Remember to include your friend's replies.

Speaking and Listening page 122

Grammar • Much, many, a lot of

★ **1** **Match the pictures (A–F) to the sentences (1–6).**

1 He has a lot of pets.   *E*
2 She has too much furniture.
3 She doesn't have much furniture.
4 He has too many pets.
5 He doesn't have many pets.
6 She has a lot of furniture.

★ **2** **Choose the correct options.**

1 How *much* / *many* movie theaters are there in this town?
2 There are a *lot of* / *much* people waiting in line.
3 There aren't *much* / *many* good movies to watch this week.
4 We don't have *much* / *many* time before the movie starts.
5 How *much* / *many* money do we need?
6 Don't take *a lot of* / *too many* food with you!

★★ **3** **Write sentences with *too much* and *too many*.**

1 She / have / old toys / her room
She has too many old toys in her room.
2 Our parents think / my sister / spend / time / on the phone
....
....
3 My mother says / I / spend / money / on shoes
....
....
4 I think my friends / spend / time / on the Internet
....
....
5 My brother says / I have / hobbies
....
....
6 There / be / salt / in the soup!
....
....

★★ **4** **Complete the conversation with these words and phrases.**

How many	~~How much~~	many	much
too many	too much		

A Those shoes are nice! ¹ *How much* did they cost?
B They were on sale for $49.50!
A You were lucky! I didn't see ²..................... shoes I liked.
B What about your shirt? Is that also new?
A Yes! Do you like it? It didn't cost ³..................... ! Only about $10.
B Really? ⁴..................... did you buy?
A I bought four!
B Wow! I wanted to buy more shoes, but my mom says I have ⁵..................... shoes already.
A My mom says I spend ⁶..................... money on clothes, too. But if it's birthday money, I can spend it on whatever I want!

Grammar Reference pages 112–113

Reading

1 Read the text quickly. Match the headings (1–3) to the paragraphs (A–C).

1 How do we recognize a shopaholic?
2 What can we do about it?
3 What exactly is the problem?

Too Much Shopping?

A ....
Some people can never get enough of shopping. They're called shopaholics, and they spend their weekends looking for bargains in shopping malls. You can often hear them comparing prices and products. But for many families, this can become a serious problem. There's often a nasty surprise at the end of the month because there isn't enough money to pay for everything.

B ....
There are many ways to discover a shopaholic. Look at their room: are there too many new things in it? Check their planner: how often do they do unnecessary shopping? Look in the garage for unopened boxes of bargains from the stores. Are they spending too much money with their credit card? If you're not sure, ask a friend for their opinion. Friends often see the situation better than we do.

C ....
A lot of people say being patient is more important than being angry. We need to help shopaholics. One of the best ideas is to offer alternatives. Help them to get interested in hobbies. Take them to the movies, theaters or concerts. Ask family and friends to give you a hand. And the next time you go shopping with them, ask them: do you really need this, or is it better for you to save the money for something more important?

2 Are the statements true (T) or false (F)?

1 A shopaholic is a person who spends too much time shopping.   *T*
2 Shopaholics don't usually spend much money.   ....
3 Inviting a shopaholic to a dance class would be a good idea.   ....
4 It's a good idea to be angry with shopaholics.   ....
5 We don't need to think much before we go shopping.   ....

Listening

1 **Listen to four radio advertisements. Number the advertisements in the order you hear them.**
14

a a chance to win a prize   ....
b free entry to a club   ....
c bargain-price furniture   *1*
d tickets by phone   ....

2 **Listen again and complete the details.**
14

1 The furniture store closes at *8 p.m.*
2 The date for Mike Springston's concert is
....
3 The bicycle store opens at
....
4 Only ....
customers can get into the club for free.

> ## Brain Trainer
>
> **Look at Grammar Reference page 112 and then put *much* and *many* into this sentence.**
>
> Too .... people
> have too .... money.
> **Now write the rule.**

Writing • A customer review

1 Read the review. Match the headings (A–D) to the paragraphs (1–4).

A What I didn't like about the restaurant   *3*
B My general opinion about the restaurant
C What I liked about the restaurant
D General information about the restaurant

Spanish Restaurants

Pepe's Taberna

"Lighting poor, restaurant noisy"

★★★☆☆   Reviewed 30 June 2014

1 Pepe's Taberna is a Spanish restaurant downtown. It's only five minutes from a bus stop, and it's open six days a week (they close on Mondays), from 12 noon until midnight. There are tables for a maximum of 80 people.

2 We went there for lunch. We ordered a big salad and paella, their special rice dish. There was a good selection of soft drinks. The salad was very fresh, and the rice was tasty. The waiters were friendly and attentive, and the prices were very reasonable.

3 However, I don't think the lighting is very good. It's too dark to see what you're eating. I also found it difficult to chat with my friends because it's a little noisy: the tables are very close together, and you can hear other people's conversations.

4 In my opinion, it's a good place for a quick lunch when you're shopping. But it's not the best place for a romantic dinner!

Visited June 2014

Was this review helpful?   **Yes**

2 Read the review again. Add these words to the correct section in column A.

attentive	~~downtown~~
fresh	friendly
good place for a quick lunch	good selection
noisy	~~noon till midnight~~
not for a romantic dinner	reasonable
six days a week	~~Spanish food~~
tasty	too dark

	A Pepe's Taberna	B My restaurant/café: ....
1 location	*downtown*	
kind of food/ cooking	*Spanish food*	
opening times	*noon till midnight*	
2 food and drink		
prices		
service		
3 atmosphere		
4 recommendation		

3 Now think of a restaurant or café you visited recently. Write the name at the top of column B. Then write information and ideas in column B.

4 Write a review. Use your ideas and information from Exercises 2 and 3.

1 ....
....
....
2 ....
....
....
3 ....
....
....
4 ....
....
....

Check 1

Grammar

1 Complete the conversation with the Present simple or Present continuous form of the verbs.

A Hi, Tom! ⁰ *Are* (be) you busy?

B Not really. I ¹........................ (check) my email, that's all.

A Anything interesting?

B One of my friends ².......................... (want) me to help him paint his room.

A Where ³........................ (he/live)?

B It's about twenty minutes by bus. But he has a swimming pool!

A That sounds OK, if you ⁴........................ (not mind) the work.

B So what ⁵........................ (you/do) now?

A I ⁶........................ (wait) for Angela. I have to talk to her.

/ 6 points

2 Complete the text with the Past simple or Past continuous form of the verbs.

Hi Mandy!

How are you? ⁰ *Did you have* (you/have) a good weekend? I have to tell you what ¹........................ (happen) yesterday! Kev and I were in that new mall near the park. We ².......................... (look) for some running shoes on sale, when we ³........................ (see) some really nice ones in a store window. The salesperson ⁴........................ (bring) them out, and Kev ⁵........................ (try) them on when this boy ⁶........................ (take) Kev's old shoes and ran away! Amazing! Kev had to buy the new shoes anyway, and I ⁷........................ (feel) sorry for him because they weren't cheap.

Write soon,

Amy

/ 7 points

3 Choose the correct options.

0 Tom loves .... cards, but I prefer video games!
  a play   **(b)** playing   **c** when play

1 Ana always gets better grades .... Albert.
  a that   **b** than   **c** to

2 Their car is old-fashioned; our car is much .... !
  a most modern
  b more modern
  c least modern

3 He's .... boy in the world.
  a the happier   **b** happiest   **c** the happiest

4 Rita bought .... jacket in the store!
  a the most expensive
  b too expensive
  c the more expensive

5 Marta is .... excited about the trip. She can't sleep!
  a enough   **b** too   **c** much

6 I'd love to buy the coat, but I don't have .... money!
  a many   **b** too   **c** enough

7 Tammie doesn't mind waiting! She has .... time.
  a a lot of   **b** much   **c** many

/ 7 points

Vocabulary

4 Choose the correct options.

0 Excuse me! How much does this .... ?
  a buy   **b** price   **(c)** cost

1 You can leave your bags on the .... at the top of the stairs.
  a yard   **b** patio   **c** landing

2 Front desk? There's no .... on my bed!
  a mirror   **b** pillow   **c** rug

3 My parents keep a lot of old stuff down in the .... .
  a ceiling   **b** basement   **c** roof

4 Paul isn't very .... insects, but I think they're really fascinating!
   a interested in   **b** good at   **c** tired of
5 This photo isn't at all clear—it's .... .
   a colorful   **b** dramatic   **c** blurry
6 The difference between the two parts of the photo is unreal. I think it's .... .
   a boring   **b** fake   **c** horrible
7 Jake doesn't have many friends. I feel .... him.
   a proud of
   b excited about
   c sorry for
8 Excuse me! The .... to pay for things is over there!
   a line   **b** ATM   **c** customer
9 There's a street market in town today! Let's see if we can find a .... .
   a coin   **b** bargain   **c** salesperson
10 I'd love to buy these shoes, but I can't .... them.
   a cost   **b** save   **c** afford

/ 10 points

Speaking

5 **Complete the conversations with these words and phrases.**

a little	Can you	give me a hand
like	~~No problem~~	Would you mind

A Can I ask you something?
B ⁰ *No problem.*
A Could you ¹....................... with these boxes?
B Sure! Where do you want them?
A I need to take them up to the attic.
B An attic? There's no attic in my apartment! What's it ²....................... ?
A Nothing special! There aren't any windows, so it's ³....................... dark. ⁴....................... opening the door first?
B No problem. Is it up these stairs?
A That's right.
B ⁵....................... go first then? I don't know the way.
A OK!

can   I don't   I'm sorry   Is it OK   mind if

A Dad! ⁶....................... if we play soccer in the backyard?
B All six of you? No, ⁷....................... . The yard isn't big enough!
A Instead, ⁸....................... we play music in the garage?
B Yes, that's all right, but I'll take the car out first.
A Do you ⁹....................... we get some pizza for dinner?
B No, ¹⁰....................... . But you better clean up the kitchen when you finish!

/ 10 points

Translation

6 **Translate the sentences.**

1 I don't have enough money to buy the CD.
   ....
2 Could you tell me where the nearest ATM is?
   ....
3 That store sells the tastiest sandwiches in town!
   ....
4 Can I borrow $20 to go to the street market?
   ....
5 I was going home on the bus when she called me.
   ....

/ 5 points

Dictation

7 **Listen and write.**
15
1 ....
2 ....
3 ....
4 ....
5 ....

/ 5 points

In the News

Vocabulary • News and media

★ **1** Label the pictures with these words and *news*.

| anchor | flash | international | ~~local~~ |
| national | paper | website | |

1 *local news*
2 ....
3 ....
4 ....
5 ....
6 ....
7 ....

★ **2** Match these words to the definitions (1–7).

| blog | current affairs show | headline |
| ~~interview~~ | journalist | podcast | report |

1 When one person asks someone else a lot of questions.   *interview*
2 Personal news and comments from an individual on a webpage.   ....
3 This is the person who finds and presents information for a newspaper.   ....
4 This is the name for the information which they present.   ....
5 This is the title for a newspaper story.   ....
6 News in the form of audio files for downloading from the Internet.   ....
7 Where people present and comment on events in the news.   ....

★ **3** Match the sentence beginnings (1–8) to the endings (a–h).

1 My sister loves clothes   *e*
2 I don't know all the details
3 We heard about a tsunami
4 She often uses her smart phone
5 My father always reads news stories
6 Opinion articles are not the same
7 I love our local newspaper
8 Sean has no time to read newspapers,

a but he often listens to podcasts.
b written by the same journalist.
c to access a news website.
d because I recognize people and places in it.
e and reads a fashion blog every week.
f on a news flash this morning.
g because I only read the headlines.
h as serious news reports.

★★ **4** Put the letters in the correct order to complete the text.

I don't mind watching the news on TV, like my parents, but I'm not interested in those ¹ *current affairs* (truncer frasifa) shows, where the news ² .... (crnaho) introduces a topic and then ³ .... (winevestir) people who know more about it. And then they all give their opinions. I only look at the newspaper for the football, but my uncle's a ⁴ .... (jolisaturn), and he says I should read the ⁵ .... (delihsane), and then the full ⁶ .... (perrot) if I want to. But it's easier for me to access a news ⁷ .... (ebistew): they have the news in pictures, on video and in podcasts, too. And the best part is the ⁸ .... (globs), because you can always find one on a topic you like.

Workbook page 119

Reading

Brain Trainer

Underline these words in the text in Exercise 1:

the news
blog
social networks
newspapers

Now do Exercise 1.

★ **1** Read the texts quickly and match the people (1–3) to their news priorities (a–c).

1 Emily
2 her brother
3 her parents

a current affairs
b pop culture
c sports

★ **2** Match the phrases (1–6) to the blanks (a–f) in the text.

1 on his cell phone, too
2 blogs if they have them
3 you can't even talk to them
4 just a few things
5 that's boring for us
6 Billy reads that regularly, too

★ **3** Are the statements true (T) or false (F)?

1 Emily prefers cartoons to news.   *T*
2 Her parents are only interested in the news on weekends.   ....
3 Her brother buys a special sports magazine.   ....
4 Billy follows his friend's news from New Delhi.   ....
5 Emily enjoys reading a friend's blog.   ....

Interview with EMILY

We asked Emily to tell us how her family get their news. This is what she said.

My mom and dad are still kind of traditional. They've always watched the news on TV at lunchtime. I mean, ᵃ _5_ , because we can't watch the cartoons on the other channel. Plus, on the weekends, they've always bought the Sunday newspapers. Then they spend half the morning reading them, so ᵇ.... !

My older brother Billy is studying biology in college, and he's always been into sports, like tennis, biking and swimming. He gets all his sports news from a specialized website, and on the weekends he gets updates on the tennis ᶜ.... . Oh, and his best friend from school is living abroad and has started a blog on life in New Delhi. So ᵈ.... .

As for me, I'm in my last year of high school. I've never been interested in the news, such as current affairs shows. I've hardly ever watched it on TV, except for ᵉ.... , like the September 11 attacks. What's important to me are my favorite singers and actors, so I follow them on the social networks, and ᶠ.... . I also started my own blog at school, so we can all keep in touch next year if we want to.

Grammar • Present perfect

★ (1) **Match the sentence beginnings (1–6) to the endings (a–f).**

1 I've been to Mexico,
2 She's had that toy
3 We've had
4 Have you ever
5 What have you
6 Where have you

a been all afternoon?
b seen on TV recently?
c had a bad dream?
d some very bad weather recently.
e since she was five.
f but I've never been to Brazil.

★ (2) **Complete the first lines of newspaper reports with the correct form of these verbs.**

appear	arrive	discover	~~escape~~
interview	open	present	record

1 A gray-haired monkey has *escaped* from the zoo.

2 A local student has .... a podcast at the radio station.

3 The mayor has .... the new theme park in the city.

4 The high school drama club has .... on the national news.

5 An American journalist has .... an award to the city.

6 Local history teachers have .... a Native American boat in the river.

7 A local student has .... Katy Perry about her new album.

8 25 Swedish students have .... in town on an exchange visit.

★ (3) **Complete the questions with the Present perfect form of these verbs. Then add the correct verb in the answers.**

1 *Have you ever climbed* (you/ever climb) a volcano? No, I *haven't*.
2 .... (your brother/ever do) the housework? No, he ....
3 .... (your parents/ever travel) to the US? No, they ....
4 .... (your family/ever visit) Paris? Yes, they ....
5 .... (you/ever buy) an expensive present? Yes, I ....
6 .... (your friend/ever lose) her cell phone? Yes, she ....

★ (4) **Put the words in the correct order.**

1 the US / wanted / Pablo / has / to / visit / always
  Pablo has always wanted to visit the US.
2 written / you / English / ever / someone / to / Have / in / ?
  ....
  ....
3 interested / comics / always / in / has / Paul / been
  ....
  ....
4 the / have / camping / weekend / gone / often / on / We
  ....
  ....
5 tried / a / Have / face / draw / you / person's / ever / to / ?
  ....
  ....
6 gone / parents / without / Have / vacation / your / ever / on / you / ?
  ....
  ....
7 been / on / your / ever / family / Has / TV / ?
  ....
  ....
8 championship / Has / a / team / ever / your / football / won / national / ?
  ....
  ....

Vocabulary • Adverbs of manner

★ **5** **Complete the conversation with the correct form of the verbs.**

A Why don't you write a report for our school blog?

B Me? I ¹ *'ve never written* (never/write) a report in my life!

A Not even in English class?

B I don't think so!

A ² .... (you/ever interview) someone?

B No. I'm not a journalist! Have you?

A Yes, I ³ .... (interview) three or four people.

B And how many reports ⁴ .... (you/do)?

A Three.

B Well, you would have to help me, then. ⁵ .... (you/think) about a person to interview?

A The school bus driver must have some interesting stories!

B OK. I'll think of the questions. Can you show me how to organize the report?

A Sure! I ⁶ .... (prepare) that for you already. Here you are!

★ **1** **Match the questions (1–5) to the answers (a–e).**

1 Does Carlos write well?   *d*
2 How fast can you run?
3 Do your friends work hard?
4 Could you speak more slowly, please?
5 How early do you want to leave?

a Sorry, I didn't realize I was speaking so fast.
b Yes, they do. Very hard!
c About 7 a.m., so we don't get there late!
d I think he writes very clearly.
e I can do a kilometer in ten minutes!

★ **2** **Complete the sentences with the opposite adverb.**

1 Jim plays the guitar well, but he sings *badly*.
2 She always drives carefully, but last night she drove ....
3 The children played happily on the floor, but their mother looked .... at the newspaper.
4 Magda reads fast in her own language, but she reads .... in English.
5 I like to get home early, but sometimes the bus is ....!
6 Mom! Don't talk so loudly on the phone! We're trying to work .... in our room.

★ **3** **Choose the correct options.**

A So, Alan. What's it like to be a blog writer?

B It's a lot of fun! I can be sitting ¹ *carelessly / quietly* at the computer when my cell phone rings ² *slowly / loudly,* and it's a friend with a good idea for a story. So I check the details ³ *early / carefully* and then upload my comments. I don't like to work too ⁴ *fast / angrily* because that's when I make mistakes.

A Do a lot of people write back?

B It depends, really. Sometimes I can wait ⁵ *patiently / sadly* at the computer and nothing happens. Other times people will ⁶ *happily / late* upload a dozen comments in ten minutes!

★★ **4** **Complete the text with the adverb form of the words.**

I was waiting ¹ *patiently* (patient) for a bus the other day when a dog appeared and started barking ² .... (loud). I'm usually a little scared of dogs, and there was no one else around. I thought ³ .... (hard) for a moment and remembered I had a cracker in my pocket. So I took it out ⁴ .... (careful) and gave it to the dog. It stopped barking immediately and wagged its tail ⁵ .... (happy). Then I touched it and talked to it, and ⁶ .... (slow) we became friends. The dog's been at my house now for three weeks!

Grammar Reference pages 114–115

Workbook page 119

Chatroom Doubt and disbelief

Speaking and Listening

★ **1** **Choose the correct options. Then listen and check.**

16

1 **A** I just saw Matt Damon at the airport!
  B *Come on now! / You're kidding!*
  A Oh yeah? Turn on the TV!

2 **A** Have you heard the news?
  B What?
  A The Yankees won the World Series!
  B *That's impossible! / Go ahead!* They lost most of their games last year!

3 **A** Hey! Our history teacher has written a book!
  B *I don't mind. / I don't believe it!*
  A She has! There's a copy in the library.

4 **A** Hi, guys! Have you seen this?
  B What is it?
  A An autograph from Cristiano Ronaldo.
  B *No problem! / No! Really?*
  A It is! My cousin works at the stadium.

5 **A** Awesome! We have a day off tomorrow!
  B *That's strange! / That's a shame!* Tomorrow's Wednesday. Why don't you check the calendar?

6 **A** Have you read the paper?
  B What happened?
  A They're closing the local gym!
  B *I'd like that! / That's ridiculous!* They only opened it last year!

★ **2** **Put the sentences in the correct order. Then listen and check.**

17

a What news? ....
b No, I'm not! Look, here's a photo! ....
c Why not? ....
d Have you heard the news? *1.*
e Yes, but it says they can't sell them. ....
f Because they don't have enough factories to build them! ....
g You're kidding! ....
h They've invented a car that runs on hydrogen! ....

★ **3** **Complete the conversation with these phrases. Then listen and check.**

18

Are you sure	I don't believe it	~~something scary~~
strange lights	that's not all	the best part

A Have you seen this story about a camel?
B No! What happened?
A This tourist was driving along when he saw ¹*something scary* on the road ahead, and made an emergency stop.
B So? That sounds normal!
A In the desert, in the middle of the night? There were ².......................... moving, too!
B No! Really?
A Yes, but ³.......................... ! He thought it was an alien from space!
B You're kidding!
A No, I'm not. That's what it says here. So he called the police.
B ⁴.......................... !
A Yes, but you haven't heard ⁵.......................... yet!
B What's that?
A They told him that police sometimes put reflectors on camels in order to prevent traffic accidents!
B Amazing! ⁶.......................... that's a real story?!

★★ **4** **Listen to the conversation in Exercise 3 again. Are the statements true (T) or false (F)?**

18

1 The driver was a local man. *F*
2 The story took place in a desert. ....
3 He was very confused about what he saw. ....
4 He called his wife. ....
5 The police explained the strange phenomenon. ....

★★ **5** **Write a conversation. Use expressions from Exercises 1–3 and this information:**

You tell a friend an amazing story you heard on TV. Your friend isn't sure if the story is real. Remember to include your friend's responses.

Speaking and Listening page 123

Grammar • Present perfect vs Past simple

★ 1 Match the beginnings of the news reports (1–5) to the endings (a–e).

1 A cat has attacked a large dog.   *d*
2 The high school's website has reached 5,000 visits.
3 A local girl has won a national blog-writing contest.
4 High school students have recorded a podcast for the city council.
5 The local newspaper has introduced a news section for teenagers.

a The school's principal said last year's maximum was only 2,400 visits.
b The paper said the section was requested by teens.
c They made the recording in English for tourists.
d When the cat found itself in a corner, it jumped on the dog.
e Elena Marquez won first prize for her fashion blog last weekend.

Girl wins national blog contest.

★ 2 Choose the correct options.

1 Steve *has broken* / *broke* his arm last weekend.
2 Oh no! My car *has disappeared* / *disappeared*!
3 Firefighters *have rescued* / *rescued* three people from an elevator yesterday.
4 My grandmother *has had* / *had* two operations.
5 A teenager *has won* / *won* this year's national chess contest.
6 Five thousand people *have attended* / *attended* the local music festival.
7 We *have lost* / *lost* our suitcases twice this year.
8 A young woman *has had* / *had* a baby in a taxi last night.

★★ 3 Write the correct form of the verbs.

A What's the most amazing newspaper story ¹*you've ever read* (you/ever read)?
B I ²........................ (not read) very many, but I ³........................ (hear) a lot of stories from other people!
A For example?
B Well, it's the silly ones I remember the best. A player ⁴........................ (have) to stay in the hospital with head injuries after a golf game.
A What happened?
B He ⁵........................ (hit) the ball really hard, the ball ⁶........................ (go) up into the sky and ⁷........................ (kill) a passing duck.
A You're kidding!
B No, no! And then the duck ⁸........................ (fall) out of the sky and ⁹........................ (strike) the player on the head!
A I don't believe it! That's the most amazing story anyone ¹⁰........................ (ever tell) me!
B Imagine that!

★★ 4 Complete the text with the correct form of these verbs.

receive	recommend	say	send
start	take	~~win~~	write

Local Teen Wins National Blog Contest

Elena Marquez, a 15-year-old from GBS High School, ¹*won* first prize in a national contest for school blogs. Elena ²........................ writing the blog two years ago when she ³........................ a camera as a present. She ⁴........................ over a thousand photos of teenagers in the street, and she ⁵........................ a fashion report every month. Her design teacher at school ⁶........................ that she enter the contest, and the organizers ⁷........................ her a text message last Monday to tell her about the prize. Her family ⁸........................ they were very proud of her.

Grammar Reference pages 114–115

Reading

1 Read the text quickly and choose the best headline.
  a Amusing Pet Monkeys
  b Humans Versus Monkeys
  c Winemaking in South Africa

AnimalNews.netcom

HOME   NEWS   BLOG   FEATURES   PHOTOS

....
by Wayne Chapman

There are many stories about conflicts between people and wild animals. We have heard about elephants in Africa eating village people's plants. There have also been reports of coyotes coming into people's yards in the US. As towns and cities use more and more land, animals have less land to live on. Usually the animals lose the competition. But in some places, the animals are slowly winning.

I've discovered an amazing story from South Africa. In one part of the country, people grow a lot of grapes for making wine. A few years ago, they began to have problems with large groups of monkeys which live in the mountains nearby. The monkeys love the sweet fruit. They ate all the grapes they wanted and then ran off to the mountains to sleep. The farmers reacted angrily, but some people defended the monkeys. "The monkeys have always lived here," they said.

But recently, the monkeys have become difficult because they get into people's homes to steal food. And they're not friendly like the monkeys on TV! One day, they even frightened a ten-year-old boy when he heard strange noises in the kitchen. People call the police, but they're not allowed to hurt the animals. So now, many families are tired of the monkeys and are selling their homes and moving away.

Imagine that! If you have any good animal stories from your town or city, please send them to me!

2 Complete the sentences with a word from the text.

1 Wild animals living near human beings often create *conflicts*.
2 The problem is often that people use more and more ....
3 The monkeys in South Africa enjoy eating ....
4 The farmers were very .... with the monkeys.
5 Now the monkeys are more ....
6 Many people are .... of the monkeys, and sell their homes.

Listening

1 Listen to the interview and choose the best answer.
19

The main subject of the interview is Steve Black's .... .
a preferences in music
b career as a musician
c concert performances

2 Listen again and choose the correct option.
19

1 Steve Black plays the *guitar* / *drums*.
2 His parents *played* / *didn't play* a lot of music.
3 When he was in school, he was a *good* / *bad* student.
4 He *writes* / *doesn't write* most of the lyrics.
5 His group has recorded *six* / *sixteen* albums.

Writing • A profile

1 Find and correct the mistakes in these phrases.
(S= spelling, G= grammar, P= punctuation)

1 wining tenis titles, and he turned proffesional
at fifteen   (S)
winning tennis titles, and he turned professional

2 he did not lose his ability   (G)

....

3 in 2008 he has also started a foundation   (G)

....

4 which is one of the balearic islands in spain   (P)

....

2 Read the text. Match the phrases (1–4) from
Exercise 1 to the blanks (a–d).

Rafael Nadal is one of the greatest tennis players
of all time. He was the first player to win the
French Open seven times, and he is currently
No. 2 in the world. I admire him for his skill and
his character, and also for the work he does
through his foundation.

Nadal was born in 1986 on the island of Mallorca,
ᵃ *4* . He went to school in his hometown of
Manacor. At the age of 12, he was already ᵇ.... .
He did not move to Barcelona to train, but stayed
in Manacor in order to finish school. In 2005, at
the age of 19, he won his first French Open title.

He continues playing tennis and winning
tournaments, but ᶜ.... to help children and
young people locally and abroad. In 2010 he
visited different educational projects in India
to show his support for the projects and help
other people become aware of them. Nadal
has become internationally famous, but ᵈ....
to understand and help other people.

3 Put these ideas in column A, according to
the paragraph they appear in.

> achievements   career   conclusion
> early life   education   ~~introduction~~
> recent activities   reasons for admiring

	A Rafael Nadal's profile	B .... profile
Paragraph 1	*introduction*	
Paragraph 2		
Paragraph 3		

4 Think of a person you would like to write about.
Add information about that person to column B.

5 Write a profile of the person you have chosen in
three paragraphs. Use your ideas and information
from Exercises 3 and 4.

....
....
....
....
....
....
....
....
....
....
....
....
....

Check

Grammar

1 **Complete the conversations with the Present perfect or Past simple form of these verbs.**

| come back | go | have to |
| hear | ~~not see~~ | stay |

A Hi, Jan! ⁰ *I haven't seen* you for a while! How are you?

B Fine, thanks!

A You're looking very tanned! ¹ .... (you) to the beach?

B Yes! We ² .... (just) from the coast. It was great!

A How long did you stay?

B Ten days. What about you?

A I ³ .... at home since school ended. My parents ⁴ .... work this month, but we're going to Spain next week! Have you been there?

B No, but I ⁵ .... about it from friends who have been. It sounds like fun.

A I'll send you a postcard!

B OK!

| know | meet | move | not talk | not write |

A Who was that?

B That was my friend Ben. I ⁶ .... to him for ages! We used to be neighbors.

A How long ⁷ .... him?

B Since we lived on the east side of town. Why?

A His face looks familiar. I think I ⁸ .... him before.

B When was that?

A At Joanna's birthday party last month.

B Joanna? Tom said I should send her an email, but I ⁹ .... it yet.

A You should do it soon, then, because she ¹⁰ .... (just) to another school.

B I didn't know that! Tell me more …

/ 10 points

2 Choose the correct options.

0 Mom says I ~~don't have to~~ / mustn't have fish for dinner. I can have chicken.

1 The school rules say that we *don't have to / mustn't* use cell phones in class.

2 It's not necessary for you to wait any longer. You *don't have to / mustn't* wait.

3 You can't wear a T-shirt here. You *have to / mustn't* wear a shirt and tie.

4 If you drive in England, remember that you *must / don't have to* drive on the left!

5 Uniforms in this school aren't essential. You *don't have to / mustn't* wear a uniform.

6 Sorry, cameras aren't allowed in here! You *don't have to / mustn't* use a camera here.

7 He *will / might* be at home, but I'm not sure.

8 It's 2:30. Tom finishes work at three o'clock, so he *won't / might* be at home now.

9 Don't worry, Mom! I promise I *'ll / might* call you when I get to the station.

10 I don't know if there's another bus. I *won't / might* have to stay the night.

/ 10 points

Vocabulary

3 **Choose the correct options.**

0 When was the last time you .... camping?
  a got   **b** did   **c** went

1 Did you .... your tan at the beach?
  a book   **b** get   **c** go

2 Have you .... your bags yet?
  a packed   **b** checked into   **c** put up

3 Isn't it your turn to .... the laundry this week?
  a clear   **b** feed   **c** do

4 Oh no! I forgot to .... the dishwasher last night.
  a mow   **b** load   **c** sweep

5 Could you please .... the dog?
  a do   **b** vacuum   **c** walk

/ 5 points

4 Choose the correct options.

Did you hear the ⁰ *report* / *blog* / *newspaper* on the radio this morning? They were talking about this 15-year-old girl who was walking down the street when two men ran out of a store in front of her. Two seconds later, a salesperson appeared, screaming ¹ *happily* / *hard* / *loudly* for help. The girl was ² *lonely* / *confused* / *guilty* for a moment, but then ran after the men! She followed them down the street and around a corner, and saw them get into a car. She wrote down the license plate number ³ *carefully* / *carelessly* / *sadly* and went back to the store. The salesperson called the police, and the men were arrested later that day. The store owner was so ⁴ *disappointed* / *fed up* / *grateful* that he gave the girl a reward. You see? The interesting stories aren't just on the ⁵ *international news* / *journalists* / *news anchors*!

/ 5 points

Speaking

5 Complete the conversations with these words or phrases.

~~an argument~~	I don't think you should
kidding	Maybe you should try
strange	Why don't you

A Jared and I had ⁰ *an argument* last night.
B That's ¹........................ . You two have always been good friends.
A Yes, I know. But he wants to date me.
B You're ²........................ !
A No, seriously! And I'm not sure about what to do.
B Well, he's a really nice guy. ³........................ going out with him.
A Yes, but it might not work.
B ⁴........................ worry about that.
A But I don't want to lose a good friend!
B ⁵........................ think it over this weekend before you make a decision?
A That's a good idea!

| get there | How long does it take | Is it far |
| to buy souvenirs | We're looking for | |

A Excuse me! Can you help us?
B Sure! What would you like to know?
A ⁶........................ the Science Museum. How can we ⁷........................ ?
B Well, you can walk or take a bus.
A ⁸........................ ?
B It's about two kilometers.
A ⁹........................ to get there?
B For young people like you, if you walk, about 15 minutes!
A And is there a good place ¹⁰........................ there?
B Yes, the museum has its own gift shop.
A So, which way do we go?

/ 10 points

Translation

6 Translate the sentences.

1 I'm sorry, the 6:30 bus just left!
....
2 You're not allowed to put up tents in this area.
....
3 You don't have to come with us if you don't want to.
....
4 Would you mind doing the dishes tonight?
....
5 You won't find any mosquitoes here.
....

/ 5 points

Dictation

7 Listen and write.

28
1 ....
2 ....
3 ....
4 ....
5 ....

/ 5 points

Grammar Reference

• Present simple and continuous

Present simple	Present continuous
He works in a café.	He's serving coffee at the moment.

Use

Present simple

We use the Present simple to talk about:

- routines and habits.
  *We **get up** late on the weekend.*

- things that are true in general.
  *I **love** surprise parties!*
  *She **hates** news shows on TV.*

Time expressions

adverbs of frequency: *every day/week/year, on Fridays, on the weekend, in the morning, at night, after school*

Present continuous

We use the Present continuous to talk about:

- things that are happening at the moment of speaking.
  *She**'s studying** in France at the moment.*

Time expressions

now, right now, just now, at the moment, today, these days

• Verb + -ing

Affirmative		
I/You/We/They He/She/It	like watching likes watching	cartoons.
Negative		
I/You/We/They He/She/It	don't like watching doesn't like watching	cartoons.
Questions		
Do I/you/we/they like watching cartoons?		
Does he/she/it like watching cartoons?		

Use

We use *like, love, enjoy, don't mind, can't stand, hate* and *prefer* + verb + *-ing* to talk about things we like or don't like doing.

Form

The verbs *like, love, enjoy, don't mind, can't stand, hate* and *prefer* are followed by a verb ending in *-ing*.
*I **don't mind watching** football on TV.*

Spelling rules

most verbs: add *-ing*   *play → playing*
verbs that end in *-e*: drop the *-e* and add *-ing* *come → coming*
verbs that end in one vowel + one consonant: double the consonant and add *-ing*   *sit → sitting*

Grammar practice • Present simple and continuous

1 Match the sentence beginnings (1–5) to the endings (a–e).

1 Bill drives a taxi,   c
2 My grandparents love sweet things,
3 Gerry travels a lot,
4 My daughter plays the cello,
5 Susan enjoys baseball,

a and today he's flying to Russia.
b and she's watching a game right now.
c and now he's waiting for a passenger.
d and she's playing in a concert right now.
e and today they're having ice cream for dessert.

2 Complete the conversation with the Present simple or Present continuous form of the verbs.

A Welcome to summer camp! There are six beds in this room!
B I (want) ¹ *want* one next to the window!
C And I (need) ² .... one near the door!
D Tina! What (you/do) ³ .... ?
B I (put) ⁴ .... my things on this bed and the one next to it.
D Why?
B Because Becky (talk) ⁵ .... to the counselor now, and I (save) ⁶ .... this bed for her.

D OK, but you (have) [7]........................ an extra pillow on your bed, and I (not have) [8]........................ any. Can you give it to me?

B Sure! Here you go!

3 Write sentences.

1 **A** What / do / Tuesdays?
What do you do on Tuesdays?

B I / usually / go / the library.

....

A What / do / today?

....

B Today / I / study / for an exam.

....

2 **A** Where / Amy / live?

....

B Her family / have / house / on the coast.

.... ,

but she / live / here with her aunt / at the moment.

....

3 **A** What / John / do / right now?

....

B He / wait / for the bus.

....

A What time / it / leave?

....

B I / be / not / sure. Maybe / it / be / late.

....

• Verb + -ing

4 Complete the text with the correct form of these verbs.

do	have	listen	live
~~look~~	take	wait	watch

We live in an apartment on the tenth floor! I like [1] *looking* out of the window at all the people down in the street, and I love [2]........................ to the rain on the walls when there's a storm. We can see the station too, and my grandfather enjoys [3]........................ all the trains come and go. But there are some things I don't like very much. I don't mind [4]........................ the dog out for a walk because I love the fresh air, but I hate [5]........................ to take the trash out to the trash cans. I prefer [6]........................ until

someone else goes down, then my brother or my parents take it out. And I can't stand [7]........................ the dishes because I always spill some water on the floor, and I have to clean it up later. I love [8]........................ so high up, because I don't feel so small anymore.

5 Put the words in the correct order.

1 doesn't / morning / mind / his / He / bed / in / making / the
He doesn't mind making his bed in the morning.

2 coffee / mother / enjoys / on / My / the / having / patio

....

3 attic / Peter / alone / hates / in / being / the / !

....

....

4 front / like / sitting / bus / at / doesn't / the / of / She / the

....

....

5 loves / fireplace / watching / the / in / Katy / the / flames

....

....

6 stand / I / to / can't / smoking / next / people / me

....

....

7 across / The / running / dogs / yard / love / the

....

....

8 blinds / Pat / with / the / sleeping / closed / prefers

....

....

Grammar Reference

• Past simple

Regular verbs: affirmative and negative		
I/You/He/She/It/We/They	lived	in an old house.
I/You/He/She/It/We/They	didn't (did not) live	in an old house.
Irregular verbs: affirmative and negative		
I/You/He/She/It/We/They	went	to New York.
I/You/He/She/It/We/They	didn't (did not) go	to New York.

Regular verbs: questions and short answers

Did I/you/he/she/it/we/they graduate from college?
Yes, I/you/he/she/it/we/they did.
No, I/you/he/she/it/we/they didn't (did not).

Irregular verbs: questions and short answers

Did I/you/he/she/it/we/they see a ghost?
Yes, I/you/he/she/it/we/they did.
No, I/you/he/she/it/we/they didn't (did not).

Wh questions

What did he do?   Where did they go?

Use

We use the Past simple to talk about:

• finished actions in the past.
  I went to the beach last weekend.

Time expressions

adverbials of past time: *last night/week/month/year, an hour/week/year ago, in 2001, in the 20th century*

• Past continuous

Affirmative		
I/He/She/It You/We/They	was talking were talking	in class.
Negative		
I/He/She/It You/We/They	wasn't (was not) talking weren't (were not) talking	in class.

Questions and short answers	
Was I/he/she/it talking in class?	Yes, I/he/she/it was. No, I/he/she/it wasn't.
Were you/we/they talking in class?	Yes, you/we/they were. No, you/we/they weren't.

Wh questions

What were they doing in the library yesterday?

Use

We use the Past continuous to talk about:

• an action in progress in the past.
  *Sean and I **were talking** about you last night!*

Time expressions

often used with particular points in past time: *yesterday morning, at 7 o'clock last Sunday, in the summer of 2014*

• Past simple vs Past continuous

long action	short action
We were taking a photo	when a man walked in front of the camera.
short action	**long action**
A man walked in front of the camera	while we were taking a photo.

Use

We often use both tenses together in order to distinguish between different actions.

• Past continuous for a longer action in progress.
• Past simple for a shorter action interrupting the other.
• *while* introduces a longer action.
• *when* introduces a shorter action.

Grammar practice • Past simple

1 **Make sentences with the Past simple.**

1 My aunt / show / us / beautiful photos / of her childhood.
My aunt showed us beautiful photos of her childhood.

2 Our cousins / take / a lot of / silly pictures / on / their school trip.
....

3 Their photos / be / blurry.
....

4 The album / be / full of / old-fashioned photos.
....

5 My friend / buy / a book / with dramatic wildlife photos.
....

6 The local newspaper / print / colorful pictures / of our school's sports teams.
....

7 The photos / of the fire / look / fake.
....

• Past continuous

2 **Complete the sentences with the Past continuous form of these verbs.**

cry	have	look	play	~~talk~~	watch

1 Mrs. Wilson *was talking* to her mother on the phone.

2 Mrs. Jones's baby .... in bed.

3 The young couple downstairs .... a boring conversation.

4 Mr. Smith .... an old-fashioned movie on TV.

5 The family .... an interesting game of cards.

6 Danny and Tom .... at photos.

3 **Make questions with the Past continuous. Complete the answers with the correct verb.**

1 Ian / clean / his room / this morning?
Was Ian cleaning his room this morning?
Yes, he *was.*

2 you / take / photography lessons / last month
....
....
No, I ....

3 neighbors / tell / funny stories / last weekend?
....
....
Yes, they ....

4 Shane / make coffee / just now?
....
No, he ....

5 the girls / read / colorful magazines?
....
No, they ....

• Past simple vs Past continuous

4 **Complete the sentences with *when* or *while*.**

1 Maria had coffee *while* Max was doing the shopping.

2 We were walking home .... we saw the fire.

3 .... the plane landed, Elena was waiting at the airport.

4 .... Richard was checking the map, I got some gas.

5 **Complete the conversations with the correct form of the verbs.**

1 A What [1] *were you doing* (you/do) when I [2] .... (arrive) just now?
B Tammi [3] .... (play) the piano, and we [4] .... (paint) in the kitchen.
A I thought the phone [5] .... (ring).
B I don't think so. We [6] .... (not hear) anything.

2 A How [7] .... (your brother/take) this blurry photo of a horse?
B He [8] .... (wait) for the right moment, when someone [9] .... (walk) into him.
A And then what [10] .... (happen)?
B While I [11] .... (help) him, the horse [12] .... (run away)!

Grammar Reference

• Comparatives and superlatives

Short adjectives	Comparatives	Superlatives
tall	taller (than)	the tallest
big	bigger (than)	the biggest
large	larger (than)	the largest
happy	happier (than)	the happiest
Long adjectives	**Comparatives**	**Superlatives**
popular	more popular (than)	the most popular
interesting	more interesting (than)	the most interesting
Irregular adjectives	**Comparatives**	**Superlatives**
good	better (than)	the best
bad	worse (than)	the worst

Use

- We use comparative adjectives to compare two people or things.
  *My hair is **longer** than Angela's.*
- We use superlative adjectives to compare one person or thing to others in a group.
  *Angela has the **shortest** hair in the class.*

Form

Short adjectives	Comparatives	Superlatives
most adjectives:	add -er small → smaller	add the + -est small → the smallest
adjectives that end in one vowel + one consonant:	double the consonant and add -er big → bigger	double the consonant and add the + -est big → the biggest
adjectives that end in -e:	add -r nice → nicer	add the + -st nice → the nicest
adjectives that end in y:	drop the y and add -ier pretty → prettier	drop the y and add the + -iest pretty → the prettiest
Long adjectives	**Comparatives**	**Superlatives**
	add more boring → more boring	add the + most boring → the most boring

- After comparative adjectives, we often use *than*.
  *Football is **more exciting than** tennis.*
- Before superlative adjectives, we use *the*.
  *Jack is **the funniest** boy in the class.*

• *Too* and *enough*

The jeans are too expensive.
The jeans aren't cheap enough.
I don't have enough money for the jeans.

Use

- We use *too* and *enough* to express an opinion about quantity (*too* = more than necessary, *not ... enough* = less than necessary).
  *It's **too** cold in here! Can you please turn the heat on?*
  *I'm **not** warm **enough**. Can you lend me a sweater?*

Form

- *too* goes before an adjective:
  *It's **too** hot in here!*
- *enough* goes after an adjective:
  *It's not cool **enough**.*
- *enough*, *too much* and *too many* go before a noun: ***enough** time*, ***too much** milk*, ***too many** cars*

• Much, many, a lot of

How much money **does** she have?	How many T-shirts **does** she have?
She has a lot of money.	She has a lot of T-shirts.
She doesn't have much/a lot of money.	She doesn't have many/a lot of T-shirts.
She has too much money.	She has too many T-shirts.

Use

- We use these words to talk about large quantities of things.
  *There were **a lot of** people/**many** cars in the street.*

Form

- We use *much* for uncountable nouns, and usually only in questions or the negative:
  *How **much** money does he have?*
  *She doesn't have **much** time.* (= She doesn't have a lot of time.)

- We use *many* for countable nouns, in the affirmative, the negative and questions:
  *They have **many** pets in the house.*
  *They don't have **many** neighbors.*
  *How **many** friends does he have?*

Grammar practice • Comparatives and superlatives

1 **Put the words in the correct order.**

1 know / most / person / the / He's / I / interesting
  He's the most interesting person I know.

2 suitcase / than / This / I / is / thought / heavier
  ....

3 here / home / weather / than / The / at / better / is
  ....

4 class / She's / in / popular / the / girl / most / the
  ....

5 car / new / old / than / is / better / the / Our / one
  ....

6 world / cousin / person / My / the / is / in / funniest / the
  ....

2 **Make sentences with the comparative or superlative.**

1 be / Poland / big / Spain?
  Is Poland bigger than Spain?

2 be / German / difficult / English?
  ....

3 Erika / tell / funny jokes / Brian.
  ....

4 That ATM / far / this one!
  ....

5 That café / have / bad sandwiches / in town!
  ....

6 Japan / be / noisy / country / in the world.
  ....

Too and enough

3 **Complete the conversation with *too* or *enough*.**

A What did you do on vacation?
B We went to the mountains.
A How was the weather?
B The first week it was [1] *too* hot to go out climbing, so we visited the town. The second week it was cool [2] .... to go out all day.
A How about the food?
B We ate out a lot. But one day we had trouble in the mountains because we didn't take [3] .... food. How about your vacation?
A We went to Paris.
B What was that like?
A Mom wanted to go to the opera, but it was [4] .... expensive. Dad wanted to walk up the Eiffel Tower, but he didn't have [5] .... energy! I wanted to visit the Louvre, but it was [6] .... big to see everything in one day. There wasn't [7] .... time.
B Yes, I know what you mean. Vacations are sometimes [8] .... tiring!

Much, many, a lot of

4 **Complete the sentences with these words.**

a lot of	How many	How much
much	too many	~~too much~~

1 I can't buy that shirt. It costs *too much*.
2 .... apples would you like to buy?
3 She's always very helpful, so she has .... friends.
4 I didn't sleep .... last night.
5 .... did you spend on your laptop?
6 I have .... books for this shelf.

Grammar Reference

• Present perfect

Regular verbs: affirmative		
I/You/We/They He/She/It	've (have) cleaned 's (has) cleaned	the house.

Regular verbs: negative		
I/You/We/They He/She/It	haven't (have not) cleaned hasn't (has not) cleaned	the house.

Irregular verbs: affirmative		
I/You/We/They He/She/It	've (have) done 's (has) done	the work.

Irregular verbs: negative		
I/You/We/They He/She/It	haven't (have not) done hasn't (has not) done	the work.

Regular verbs				
Have Has	I/you/we/they he/she/it	ever	visited	Arizona?

Irregular verbs				
Have Has	I/you/we/they he/she/it	ever	seen	a snake?

Short answers
Yes, I/you/we/they have. / No, I/you/we/they haven't. Yes, he/she/it has. / No, he/she/it hasn't.

Use

We use the Present perfect to talk about:

- actions or events that happened at an unspecified time in the past, but are relevant to the present.
  John has visited China. (but we don't know when)

- with *ever*, we ask questions about personal experiences.
  Have you ever listened to a podcast?

- with *never*, we talk about experiences we have not had.
  No, I haven't. I've never listened to a podcast—but I've visited news websites!

• Present perfect vs Past simple

Present perfect	Past simple
A helicopter has landed in the jungle.	A plane crashed in the mountains *last Saturday*.
Have you ever seen a helicopter?	Did it crash because of the weather?
I've never flown in a helicopter.	Rescue teams located the plane on *Sunday morning*.

Use

We use the Past simple to talk about:

- actions or events that happened at a specific time in the past.

Time expressions

Present perfect: *ever, never, before, recently, in my life*
Past simple: *last night/week/year, five hours/days/ months ago, in 2012*

Grammar practice • Present perfect

1 **Rewrite the sentences. Put the words in parentheses in the correct place.**

1 Have you been to North America? (ever)
   Have you ever been to North America?

2 Which African countries he visited? (has)
   ....
   ....

3 Has your brother anything for the school blog? (written)
   ....
   ....

4 We've watched a current affairs show. (never)
   ....
   ....

5 They answered all of today's emails. (have)
   ....
   ....

6 I'm sorry, but I finished my report. (haven't)
   ....
   ....

2 Write questions for the underlined answers.

1 He's made the sandwiches already.
What has he made?
2 They've been to China.
....
3 I've never won a prize in the lottery!
....
4 My aunt has two girls; she's never had a baby boy!
....
5 Patricia's not here; she's gone to Italy.
....
6 He's interviewed Lady Gaga three times.
....
7 We've finally finished reading the news.
....
8 They've written another excellent report.
....

• Present perfect vs Past simple

3 Match the questions (1–5) to the answers (a–e).

1 Have you ever written a blog?   *a*
2 Have you ever been on TV?
3 Have you ever recorded a podcast?
4 Have you ever bought a newspaper?
5 Have you ever watched the local news?

a Yes, I wrote a travel blog for my class trip in March.
b Yes, I have. We recorded it in science class.
c No, I haven't. I read the news on a website.
d Yes. I've watched it on TV and on my laptop.
e No, but my friend was on a talent show last year.

4 Choose the correct options.

1 Kathy *has written* / ⟨wrote⟩ a letter to the newspaper last weekend.
2 That's my mom's new car. She *bought* / *has bought* it last week.
3 Where's Isabel? I *haven't seen* / *didn't see* her recently.
4 My parents *have gone* / *went* home half an hour ago.
5 Alex says he *never had* / *has never had* a pet.
6 What time *did you get up* / *have you gotten up* this morning?

5 Write sentences.

1 I / go to / beach / but / I / never go to / mountains.
I've been to the beach, but I've never been to the mountains.
2 In 2013 we / visit Scotland / and / write / travel blog.
....
....
3 We / download / podcast / but / not be / very interesting.
....
....
4 In science class / we / write / three reports / this week.
....
....
5 Amy / interview / two local journalists / for the school magazine.
....
....

6 Complete the conversation with the correct form of these verbs.

can not	catch	find	never hear
print	~~read~~	turn on	think

A [1] *Have you read* this report in the paper?
B I don't know! What's it about?
A A man was out fishing in the ocean one day when he [2] .... a fish.
B And?
A On the way home, he [3] .... he heard some strange music in the car.
B Was the car radio not on?
A No! That's why he [4] .... understand where the music was coming from.
B So what happened?
A When he cut the fish open, he [5] .... an MP3 player in its stomach!
B That's impossible! I [6] .... such a silly story! [7] .... the fish .... the MP3 player?!
A This paper [8] .... some very strange reports recently.

Vocabulary

Home Sweet Home

Unit vocabulary

1 **Translate the words.**

Rooms and parts of the house

attic ....

balcony ....

basement ....

ceiling ....

driveway ....

fireplace ....

floor ....

garage ....

hallway ....

landing ....

office ....

patio ....

roof ....

stairs ....

wall ....

yard ....

2 **Translate the words.**

Furniture and household objects

alarm clock ....

armchair ....

blind ....

bookcase ....

closet ....

comforter ....

curtains ....

cushions ....

dresser ....

mirror ....

pillow ....

rug ....

vase ....

Vocabulary extension

3 **Match the photos to these words. Use your dictionary if necessary. Write the words in English and in your language.**

| chimney | elevator | faucets | ~~towel~~ | sink |

1 ....
....

2 ....
....

3 ....
....

4 .... *towel* ....
....

5 ....
....

Vocabulary

What's the Story?

Unit vocabulary

1 Translate the words.

Adjectives to describe pictures

beautiful ....

blurry ....

boring ....

colorful ....

dark ....

dramatic ....

fake ....

funny ....

horrible ....

interesting ....

old-fashioned ....

silly ....

2 Translate the words.

Adjective + preposition

afraid of ....

angry with ....

bad at ....

bored with ....

excited about ....

good at ....

interested in ....

popular with ....

proud of ....

sorry for ....

tired of ....

Vocabulary extension

3 Match the photos to these words. Use your dictionary if necessary. Write the words in English and in your language.

> annoyed about   ~~disappointed with~~   mysterious
> scary   surprised at

1 ....
....

2 ....
....

3 ......*disappointed with*.......
....

4 ....
....

5 ....
....

Vocabulary

It's a Bargain!

Unit vocabulary

1 Translate the words.

Shopping nouns

ATM ....
bargain ....
bill ....
change ....
coin ....
customer ....
line ....
mall ....
market stand ....
price ....
products ....
sale ....
salesperson ....
shopping basket ....
vendor ....

2 Translate the words.

Money verbs

afford ....
borrow ....
buy ....
cost ....
earn ....
lend ....
pay by credit card ....
pay in cash ....
save ....
sell ....
spend ....
win ....

Vocabulary extension

3 Match the photos to these words. Use your dictionary if necessary. Write the words in English and in your language.

bar code	discount	receipts	refund	~~sell-by date~~

1 ....
....

2 ....
....

3 .... *sell-by date* ....
....

4 ....
....

5 ....
....

Vocabulary

In the News

Unit vocabulary

1 Translate the words.

News and media

blog ....
current affairs show
....
headline ....
international news ....
interview (n, v) ....
journalist ....
local news ....
national news ....
news anchor ....
news flash ....
newspaper ....
news website ....
podcast ....
report (n, v) ....

2 Translate the words.

Adverbs of manner

angrily ....
badly ....
carefully ....
carelessly ....
early ....
fast ....
happily ....
hard ....
late ....
loudly ....
patiently ....
quietly ....
sadly ....
slowly ....
well ....

Vocabulary extension

3 Match the photos and pictures to these words. Use your dictionary if necessary. Write the words in English and in your language.

> cartoon strip   entertainment guide   front page
> proudly   ~~quickly~~

1 ....
....

2 ....
....

3 ....
....

4 .... *quickly* ....

5 ....
....

Speaking and Listening

Describing a place

• Speaking

1 **Complete the text with these phrases.**
42 **Then listen and check.**

big fireplace	big windows	closet
comfortable	~~pretty new~~	very narrow
wooden ceilings		

Welcome to the old castle! This is the main entrance, between these two towers. The towers look a little strange, because many parts of them are ¹*pretty new*. The windows are ²....................., and they don't have any glass. If we go inside, we can see the main buildings on the left. The building with the really ³........................ is the Great Hall. It has six fireplaces, and tables and chairs for a hundred people! The building opposite the Hall is for the royal apartments. The apartments have high ⁴........................, walls covered in special cloths called tapestries, and rugs on the floor. Each room has a ⁵........................ to keep people warm and, of course, a very ⁶........................ bed. There isn't very much furniture, usually just a dresser and a ⁷........................ .

2 **Complete the conversation with these phrases.**
43 **Then listen and check.**

| kind of small | ~~like~~ | original |
| uncomfortable | very expensive | what |

A What's that new café ¹*like*?

B You mean the Skyspace?

A Yes, that's it. I've heard it has some really ²........................ decoration.

B That's what Cindy says, too. She told me it has a blue ceiling with stars painted on it.

A Wow! So ³........................ are the tables and chairs like?

B The tables are painted yellow like the sun, but they're ⁴........................ .

A OK!

B And the chairs look like stars, but they're really ⁵........................ .

A Huh. What about the prices?

B Cindy says things are ⁶........................ . A coffee costs three bucks, for example.

A Yikes! Forget it! We'll go to the café at the station.

• Listening

3 **Listen and complete the sentences.**
44
1 Laura is staying in a hotel on the ....

2 She's going on vacation with her ....

3 Frank and Laura can see the hotel in some ....

4 The rooms have a .... with a table and chairs.

5 Frank isn't interested in playing .... at this kind of hotel.

6 Frank doesn't like playing .... at school.

7 There's a club for .... at the hotel.

4 **Listen again. Who says these phrases? Write F**
44 **for Frank or L for Laura.**

1 What's it like? ....

2 look at the view! ....

3 four tennis courts ....

4 Not at school! ....

5 What about nightlife? ....

6 That sounds like fun! ....

Speaking and Listening

Permission

• Speaking

1 **Match the questions (1–6) to the answers (a–f).**
45 **Then listen and check.**

1 Can I stay overnight at Maria's house?   c
2 Do you mind if we park here?
3 Is it OK if I wear jeans?
4 Can we invite some friends for the weekend?
5 Do you mind if I come home late?
6 Is it OK if we make pizza?

a No, I'm sorry, it isn't. You need something more formal.
b No, I don't mind. But not later than eleven o'clock.
c Yes, you can. But call me in the morning.
d Go ahead! I'll have one with four cheeses.
e No, you can't. We're going away this weekend.
f Yes, I do! This is the entrance to a garage!

2 **Complete the conversation with these phrases.**
46 **Then listen and check.**

| Can we do | Do you mind | ~~Go ahead~~ |
| I'm sorry | take photos | Yes, of course |

A Bankside Vacation Rentals! Can I help you?
B I'd like to ask a few questions, please.
A ¹ *Go ahead*!
B Is it OK if we ²......................... of the apartment?
A ³......................... ! Most people take vacation pictures.
B That's fine! And what about uploading them on the Internet? ⁴......................... that?
A Sure. That's not a problem.
B Great! And what about pets? ⁵......................... if we bring a pet?
A What kind of pet? ⁶......................... , we can't accept large animals.
B It's just a cat.
A Yes, that's OK, but only on the balcony.
B Thank you!

• Listening

3 **Listen and choose the correct options.**
47
1 The mother is happy / *unhappy* for the boy to see the photos.
2 The photos are in *a box* / *an album*.
3 The grandma died in *1970* / *1980*.
4 The grandparents were born *before* / *after* the war.
5 The *grandpa* / *grandma* was an electrician.

4 **Listen again. Put the phrases in the order**
47 **you hear them.**

a in those days   ....
b might get lost   ....
c When did they live? ....
d just before   ....
e take a look at   .1.

Speaking and Listening

Asking for help

• Speaking

1 **Put the sentences in the correct order.**
48 **Then listen and check.**

a Three. What do you think of this one? ....

b Well, can you hold these while I try the other ones? ....

c Yeah, I think so, too. ....

d Lisa! Could you give me a hand with these shirts? *1*

e It looks too big for you, actually. ....

f Sure. What do you want me to do? ....

g OK! How many do you have? ....

2 **Complete the conversation with these words.**
49 **Then listen and check.**

can't	cost	~~give~~	lending
looking	No	price	

A Carlos! Could you ¹*give* me a hand at the market? I don't speak much Spanish!

B ² .... problem! What are you ³ .... for?

A Some T-shirts, I think.

B OK. Do you see any that you like?

A Those look all right. Could you ask how much they ⁴ .... ?

B Sure … The vendor says they're $10 each.

A That's a good ⁵ .... ! I'll take five of them, but in different colors.

B That's easy. There you go!

A Oh no! I only have $30! I forgot to go to the bank! Would you mind ⁶ .... me $20 to pay for the T-shirts?

B Sorry, I ⁷ .... ! I didn't bring my wallet. But there's an ATM just around the corner. We can go there.

A OK, let's do that!

• Listening

3 **Listen and choose the correct options.**
50 1 The girl needs help with her *housework* / *homework*.

2 The group *can* / *can't* afford hotels.

3 The problem with camping is the *location* / *weather*.

4 The best alternative is *camping* / *a youth hostel*.

5 The girl *has* / *doesn't have* her cell phone with her.

4 **Listen again. Put the phrases in the order**
50 **you hear them.**

a Could you think of a better way? ....

b she forgot to bring it back ....

c Everyone can afford that! ....

d Check how much you have to pay ....

e Are you busy? *1*

f I'll check that out now. ....

Speaking and Listening

Doubt and disbelief

● Speaking

1 **Put the sentences in the correct order.**
51 **Then listen and check.**

a What are you reading? .*1*..
b And what does it say? ....
c Let me check. Oops! I've sent 45! ....
d It says that high school students send
about 30 text messages a day. ....
e A magazine report about young people
and cell phones. ....
f I don't believe it! I've only sent about
20 messages today. And you? ....

2 **Complete the conversation with these phrases.**
52 **Then listen and check.**

a strange figure	~~believe~~	impossible
just a statue	kidding	No! Really
That's strange		

A Have you read this report about a ghost
in the local museum?
B I don't ¹ *believe* it!
A It's been in the national news as well.
B ² .... ? What's the story?
A It says people have seen ³ ....
in the museum. And that there have been
reports like this for many years.
B Well, I've never heard of them! Does the
figure move, or is it ⁴ .... ?
A They say it moves around different parts of
the museum.
B That's ⁵ .... ! You would see it
on the video cameras!
A But there aren't any video cameras!
B ⁶ .... ! Most museums have them.
Listen! Why don't we spend the night there
with a camera?
A You're ⁷ .... ! They wouldn't let us
do that!

● Listening

3 **Listen and match the key words (1–5)**
53 **to the words (a–e).**

1 vampire   a dates
2 Germany   b Happy Birthday
3 lose   c semifinals
4 dog   d trailer
5 concert   e match

4 **Listen again. Put the phrases in the order**
53 **you hear them.**

a What about France? ....
b You're kidding! ....
c Anything else? ....
d That's news to me! ....
e I expected that! .*1*..
f I don't believe it! ....

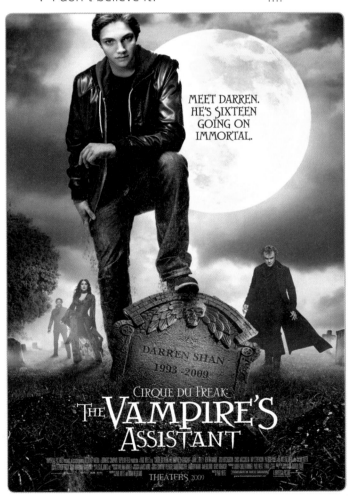

MEET DARREN.
HE'S SIXTEEN
GOING ON
IMMORTAL.

DARREN SHAN
1993 -2009

CIRQUE DU FREAK:
THE VAMPIRE'S
ASSISTANT

THEATERS 2009

Pronunciation

Consonants

Symbol	Example	Your examples
/p/	park	
/b/	big	
/t/	toy	
/d/	dog	
/k/	car	
/g/	good	
/tʃ/	chair	
/dʒ/	jeans	
/f/	farm	
/v/	visit	
/θ/	three	
/ð/	they	
/s/	swim	
/z/	zoo	
/ʃ/	shop	
/ʒ/	television	
/h/	hot	
/m/	map	
/n/	notes	
/ŋ/	sing	
/l/	laptop	
/r/	room	
/y/	yellow	
/w/	watch	

Vowels

Symbol	Example	Your examples
/ɪ/	rich	
/ɛ/	egg	
/æ/	rat	
/ɑ/	job	
/ʌ/	fun	
/ʊ/	put	
/i/	eat	
/eɪ/	gray	
/aɪ/	my	
/ɔɪ/	boy	
/u/	boot	
/oʊ/	note	
/aʊ/	now	
/ɪr/	hear	
/ɛr/	hair	
/ɑr/	star	
/ɔ/	dog	
/ʊr/	tour	
/ɔr/	door	
/ə/	among	
/ɚ/	shirt	

Pronunciation practice

Unit 1 • /v/, /w/ and /b/

(1) Listen and repeat.

69   1 We will drive these five vans down
      Bay Avenue.
    2 Will you wait for me while I'm away?
    3 Meet Bill at the library, and bring your
      bicycle, too!
    4 Put the books in the bookcase and the bike
      on the balcony.
    5 Put the heavy vases on the living room floor.
    6 We always travel abroad for our winter break.

(2) Put words from Exercise 1 in the correct column.
69   **Then listen again and check.**

/v/	/w/	/b/
drive	we	Bay

Unit 2 • Sentence stress

(1) Listen and repeat the stressed words.

70   1 What – do
    2 What – do – work
    3 What – doing
    4 What – doing – morning
    5 doing – homework – room
    6 wasn't – games – laptop

(2) Listen again and write the sentences.

70   1 ....
    2 ....
    3 ....
    4 ....
    5 ....
    6 ....

(3) Listen again and repeat the complete sentences.
70

Unit 3 • /ɔ/ and /oʊ/

(1) Listen and repeat.

71   1 We bought all the donuts in the store!
    2 I don't know!
    3 This coat is too short for me.
    4 No cell phones in here!
    5 He lost his dog in the forest.
    6 Don't go home now!

(2) Put words from Exercise 1 in the correct column.
71   **Then listen again and check.**

/ɔ/	/oʊ/
bought	donuts

Unit 4 • /æ/ and /ɑ/

(1) Listen and repeat.

72   1 You can't charge your laptop batteries
      in the café!
    2 Carry the backpacks please, Sam!
    3 They ran into a traffic jam on the way to
      the park.
    4 That's the first album she sang with the band.

(2) Put words from Exercise 1 in the correct column.
72   **Then listen again and check.**

/æ/	/ɑ/
can't	charge

Irregular Verb List

Verb	Past Simple	Past Participle
be	was/were	been
become	became	become
begin	began	begun
break	broke	broken
bring	brought	brought
build	built	built
buy	bought	bought
can	could	been able
catch	caught	caught
choose	chose	chosen
come	came	come
cost	cost	cost
cut	cut	cut
do	did	done
draw	drew	drawn
drink	drank	drunk
drive	drove	driven
eat	ate	eaten
fall	fell	fallen
feed	fed	fed
feel	felt	felt
fight	fought	fought
find	found	found
fly	flew	flown
forget	forgot	forgotten
get	got	gotten
give	gave	given
go	went	gone/been
have	had	had
hear	heard	heard
hold	held	held
keep	kept	kept
know	knew	known
leave	left	left
lend	lent	lent

Verb	Past Simple	Past Participle
light	lit	lit
lose	lost	lost
make	made	made
mean	meant	meant
meet	met	met
pay	paid	paid
put	put	put
read /rid/	read /rɛd/	read /rɛd/
ride	rode	ridden
ring	rang	rung
run	ran	run
say	said	said
see	saw	seen
sell	sold	sold
send	sent	sent
shine	shone	shone
show	showed	shown
sing	sang	sung
sit	sat	sat
sleep	slept	slept
speak	spoke	spoken
spend	spent	spent
stand	stood	stood
steal	stole	stolen
swim	swam	swum
take	took	taken
teach	taught	taught
tell	told	told
think	thought	thought
throw	threw	thrown
understand	understood	understood
wake	woke	woken
wear	wore	worn
win	won	won
write	wrote	written

My Assessment Profile Starter Unit

1 **What can I do? Mark (✓) the options in the table.**

⏪ = I need to study this again.   ⏸ = I'm not sure about this.   ▶ = I'm happy with this.   ⏩ = I do this very well.

		⏪	⏸	▶	⏩
Vocabulary (pages 4–7)	• I can use common verbs correctly. • I can use prepositions correctly. • I can talk about everyday objects. • I can talk about school subjects. • I can talk about numbers and dates. • I can use opinion adjectives correctly.				
Reading (page 9)	• I can understand profiles on a school intranet page.				
Grammar (pages 4–7)	• I can use all forms of *to be* in the Present simple. • I can use all forms of *have* in the Present simple. • I can use the possessive *'s* correctly. • I can tell the difference between possessive*'s* and the contraction *'s*. • I can use subject and object pronouns correctly. • I can use possessive adjectives correctly. • I can use indefinite pronouns correctly. • I can use the Present simple correctly. • I can use adverbs of frequency correctly. • I can use *was/were* correctly.				
Speaking (page 8)	• I can ask for and give personal information.				
Listening (page 8)	• I can understand conversations about personal information.				
Writing (page 9)	• I can write a personal profile.				

2 **What new words and expressions can I remember?**

words ....

expressions ....

3 **How can I practice other new words and expressions?**

record them on my MP3 player ☐   write them in a notebook ☐
practice them with a friend ☐   translate them into my language ☐

4 **What English have I learned outside class?**

	words	expressions
on the radio		
in songs		
in movies		
on the Internet		
on TV		
with friends		

My Assessment Profile Unit (1)

1 What can I do? Mark (✓) the options in the table.

⏪ = I need to study this again.   ⏸ = I'm not sure about this.   ▶ = I'm happy with this.   ⏩ = I do this very well.

		⏪	⏸	▶	⏩
Vocabulary (pages 10 and 13)	• I can talk about rooms and parts of the house. • I can talk about furniture and household objects.				
Pronunciation (page 13)	• I can understand and say correctly the sounds /v/, /w/ and /b/.				
Reading (pages 11 and 16)	• I can understand articles about houses and rooms.				
Grammar (pages 12 and 15)	• I can use the Present simple and Present continuous correctly. • I can use verbs with the -ing form correctly.				
Speaking (pages 14 and 15)	• I can describe a place.				
Listening (page 16)	• I can understand a person describing her room.				
Writing (page 17)	• I can link similar and contrasting ideas. • I can write a description of a room.				

2 What new words and expressions can I remember?

words ....

expressions ....

3 How can I practice other new words and expressions?

record them on my MP3 player ☐   write them in a notebook ☐

practice them with a friend ☐   translate them into my language ☐

4 What English have I learned outside class?

	words	expressions
on the radio		
in songs		
in movies		
on the Internet		
on TV		
with friends		

My Assessment Profile Unit

1 **What can I do? Mark (✓) the options in the table.**

 = I need to study this again. ❚❚ = I'm not sure about this. ▶ = I'm happy with this. ▶▶ = I do this very well.

		◀◀	❚❚	▶	▶▶
Vocabulary (pages 20 and 23)	• I can use adjectives to describe pictures. • I can use adjectives with prepositions.				
Pronunciation (page 23)	• I can hear stressed words in sentences and say sentences with the correct stress.				
Reading (pages 21 and 26)	• I can understand descriptions of pictures and stories behind the pictures.				
Grammar (pages 22, 23 and 25)	• I can use the Past simple and Past continuous correctly.				
Speaking (pages 24 and 25)	• I can ask for and give permission.				
Listening (page 26)	• I can understand people talking about a famous photo.				
Writing (page 27)	• I can locate people and things in a picture. • I can write a description of a picture.				

2 **What new words and expressions can I remember?**

words ....

expressions ....

3 **How can I practice other new words and expressions?**

record them on my MP3 player ☐   write them in a notebook ☐

practice them with a friend ☐   translate them into my language ☐

4 **What English have I learned outside class?**

	words	expressions
on the radio		
in songs		
in movies		
on the Internet		
on TV		
with friends		

My Assessment Profile   Unit

1 What can I do? Mark (✓) the options in the table.

◄◄ = I need to study this again.   ❚❚ = I'm not sure about this.   ► = I'm happy with this.   ►► = I do this very well.

		◄◄	❚❚	►	►►
Vocabulary (pages 30 and 33)	• I can talk about shopping. • I can use shopping nouns and money verbs.				
Pronunciation (page 33)	• I can understand and say correctly the sounds /ɔ/ and /oʊ/.				
Reading (pages 31 and 36)	• I can understand articles about shopping.				
Grammar (pages 32 and 35)	• I can use comparatives and superlatives correctly. • I can use *too* and *enough* correctly. • I can use *much, many* and *a lot of* correctly.				
Speaking (pages 34 and 35)	• I can ask for help and respond.				
Listening (page 36)	• I can understand a radio news report.				
Writing (page 37)	• I can express my opinion in writing. • I can write a customer review.				

2 What new words and expressions can I remember?

words ....

expressions ....

3 How can I practice other new words and expressions?

record them on my MP3 player ☐   write them in a notebook ☐

practice them with a friend ☐   translate them into my language ☐

4 What English have I learned outside class?

	words	expressions
on the radio		
in songs		
in movies		
on the Internet		
on TV		
with friends		

My Assessment Profile Unit

1. **What can I do? Mark (✓) the options in the table.**

⏪ = I need to study this again.   ⏸ = I'm not sure about this.   ▶ = I'm happy with this.   ⏩ = I do this very well.

		⏪	⏸	▶	⏩
Vocabulary (pages 44 and 47)	• I can talk about news and the media. • I can use adverbs of manner.				
Pronunciation (page 47)	• I can understand and say correctly the sounds /æ/ and /ɑ/.				
Reading (pages 45 and 50)	• I can understand newspaper and magazine reports.				
Grammar (pages 46 and 49)	• I can use the Present perfect correctly. • I know when to use the Present perfect and when to use the Past simple.				
Speaking (pages 48 and 49)	• I can express doubt and disbelief.				
Listening (page 50)	• I can understand different people talking about the news.				
Writing (page 51)	• I can check spelling, punctuation and grammar. • I can write a profile.				

2. **What new words and expressions can I remember?**

words   ....

expressions   ....

3. **How can I practice other new words and expressions?**

record them on my MP3 player   ☐   write them in a notebook   ☐
practice them with a friend   ☐   translate them into my language   ☐

4. **What English have I learned outside class?**

	words	expressions
on the radio		
in songs		
in movies		
on the Internet		
on TV		
with friends		

Notes

Notes

Notes

Notes

Pearson Education Limited
Edinburgh Gate
Harlow
Essex CM20 2JE
England
and Associated Companies throughout the world.

www.pearsonelt.com/moveit

© Pearson Education Limited 2015

The right of Fiona Beddall, Jayne Wildman and Joe McKenna to be identified as the authors of this work has been asserted by them in accordance with the Copyright, Designs and Patents Act, 1988.

First published 2015
Eighth impression 2020
Set in 10.5/12.5pt LTC Helvetica Neue Light
ISBN: 978-1-2921-0135-4
Printed and bound by L.E.G.O. S.p.A. (Italy)

Acknowledgements

We are grateful to the following for permission to reproduce copyright material:
Article 1.1 adapted from www.minihousebuilder.com; Article 6.7 adapted from www.bullyingcanada.ca

Photo Acknowledgements

The publisher would like to thank the following for their kind permission to reproduce their photographs:

(Key: b-bottom; c-centre; l-left; r-right; t-top)

Students' Book:
Alamy Images: AAD Worldwide Travel Images 20tr, CountrySideCollection - Homer Sykes 64tl, imagebroker 20cl, David L. Moore 45, Adrian Sherratt 27b; **Corbis:** Bettmann 61, Destinations 63t, Simon Jarratt 27t, Ocean 20tl, David Turnley 50; **Fotolia.com:** Pablo H. Caridad 19tr, Aleksandar Jocic 37, Monia 20bl, 42, Pascal Rateau 19cr; **Getty Images:** 2009 Blixah 7, 36r, 64tr, 64br, Maxine Adcock 36l, DreamPictures 47, Tony Eveling 21cl, Gamma-Rapho 53tr, 53br, Scott MacBride 20br, Regine Mahaux 12, Michael Nichols 21bl, Alberto E. Rodriguez 53tl, Aurora Rodriguez 21cr, Time & Life Pictures 26l, Time Life Pictures 26tr, UNICEF 51; **Pearson Education Ltd:** Gareth Boden 8, 9tl, 9tr, 9bl, 9br, 14, 24, 34, 48, 58tl, 58br, 59bl, 60tl, 60tr; **Press Association Images:** Manchester City FC / Ed Garvey 64bl; **Rex Features:** Albanpix Ltd 29tl, 29tr, 29b, c.Warner Br / Everett 52, The World of Sports SC 26br; **Shutterstock.com:** col 62tr, Louise Cukrov 19tl, Deymos.HR 31l, K. Geijer 62cr, Andrew Lam 62br, littleny 31r, Pressmaster 56, rSnapshotPhotos 62bl; **SuperStock:** Prisma 19br, 20cr, The Irish Image Collection 63b; **www.tumbleweedhouses.com:** 11

Workbook:
Alamy Images: allesalltag 118b, Archimage 89t, Arco Images GmbH 104, blickwinkel 81b, Christine Nichols 81c, SuperStock 89b, Colin Underhill 118tr, Tony Watson 120, Young-Wolff Photography 99t; **Corbis:** cultura / Monty Rakusen 117cl, Bob Krist 121; **Fotolia.com:** 127-131, withGod 99b; **FotoLibra:** Mkimages 116b; **Getty Images:** Digital Vision / Paul Burns 117cr, Lifesize / Maria Teijeiro 87, Stockbyte / Jae Rew 94, StockImage / Bernard Jaubert 81t, The Image Bank / Britt Erlanson 117b;

Press Association Images: AP / Brynjar Gauti 86; **Rex Features:** Sipa / Di Crollalanza 105, Ray Tang 118cr; **Shutterstock.com:** CristinaMuraca 73, Dean Drobot 103, Jaimie Duplass 118cl, Francois Etienne du Plessis 119b, Kitch Bain 116tr, Kokhanchikov 116tl, Monkey Business Images 77t, photobar 119t, Photoseeker 116cl, Rechitan Sorin 116cr, Heidi Schneider 117tr, THPStock 118tl, Tupungato 122, Alex Yeung 78, Olena Zaskochenko 77b; **SuperStock:** Scott Stulberg 117tl; **The Kobal Collection:** Universal Pictures 123

Cover images: *Front:* **Shutterstock.com**: Galina Barskaya

All other images © Pearson Education

Every effort has been made to trace the copyright holders and we apologise in advance for any unintentional omissions. We would be pleased to insert the appropriate acknowledgement in any subsequent edition of this publication.

Illustrated by

Students' Book:
Andy Robert Davies; Paula Franco; Peskimo; Zara Picken; Gary Rose; Ben Steers.

Workbook:
Moreno Chiacchiera; Peskimo; Paula Franco